Ranking On Google: How To Rank on the First Page

Roy Hendershot

Published by Roy Hendershot, 2024.

While every precaution has been taken in the preparation of this book, the publisher assumes no responsibility for errors or omissions, or for damages resulting from the use of the information contained herein.

RANKING ON GOOGLE: HOW TO RANK ON THE FIRST PAGE

First edition. June 10, 2024.

Copyright © 2024 Roy Hendershot.

Written by Roy Hendershot.

Table of Contents

Chapter 1: Understanding Google's Algorithm 1

Chapter 2: Keyword Research Mastery 8

Chapter 3: Crafting High-Quality Content 15

Chapter 4: On-Page SEO Techniques 22

Chapter 5: Technical SEO Fundamentals 29

Chapter 6: Building Quality Backlinks 36

Chapter 7: Local SEO Strategies 43

Chapter 8: Content Marketing and SEO 50

Chapter 9: Social Media and SEO 57

Chapter 10: Measuring and Analyzing SEO Performance 64

Chapter 11: Voice Search Optimization 71

Chapter 12: Mobile SEO Best Practices 77

Chapter 13: E-commerce SEO Strategies 82

Chapter 14: SEO for Blog Growth 89

Chapter 15: Advanced SEO Techniques 95

Chapter 1: Understanding Google's Algorithm

Google's algorithm is like the secret recipe for the world's most popular search engine. Just like a chef keeps their special ingredients a secret, Google keeps its algorithm details under wraps. But don't worry, we can still figure out the main ingredients that make up this recipe. At the heart of Google's search engine is a complex system that decides which websites show up when you type something into the search bar. This system, called an algorithm, sorts through billions of web pages to find the most relevant results for you.

The history of Google's algorithm changes is like a roller coaster ride. Google started with a simple idea: show the most relevant pages first. Over the years, this idea has become more complex with frequent updates and improvements. Major updates like Panda, Penguin, and Hummingbird have shaped the way websites are ranked today. Each update targets different aspects of web pages, such as content quality, backlinks, and user experience. These changes aim to make search results more accurate and useful for users.

Keywords are one of the main ingredients in Google's algorithm. When you search for something, Google looks for words that match your query in web pages. These words, known as keywords, help Google understand what a page is about. But it's not just about matching words; Google also considers how relevant those words are to what you're searching for. That's why simply stuffing a page with keywords doesn't work anymore. You need to use them naturally and in the right context.

User intent is another key factor in Google's algorithm. When you type a query, Google tries to understand what you really want. Are you looking for information, trying to buy something, or just browsing? Understanding this intent helps Google show the most relevant results. For instance, if you search for "best pizza," Google knows you're likely looking for places to eat pizza rather than recipes or history about pizza. This understanding of user intent makes search results more accurate and useful.

Backlinks are like votes of confidence for your website. When other sites link to yours, it signals to Google that your content is valuable and trustworthy. Not all backlinks are created equal, though. Links from reputable sites carry more weight than those from unknown or spammy sites. Building a strong backlink profile can significantly boost your rankings. But remember, it's about quality, not quantity. A few links from authoritative sites are better than many from low-quality ones.

Content quality and relevance play a crucial role in Google's algorithm. High-quality content that provides value to users ranks higher. This means your content should be well-written, informative, and engaging. It should answer the questions users are asking and provide them with useful information. Relevance is also important. Your content should match the search queries it's targeting. If your page is about gardening tips, it should provide detailed and accurate information about gardening, not just general information.

Mobile-first indexing means Google primarily uses the mobile version of your site for ranking and indexing. With more people using smartphones to browse the web, Google wants to ensure users have a good experience on mobile devices. This shift means your site needs to be mobile-friendly to rank well. Responsive design, fast loading times, and easy navigation are key factors. If your site isn't optimized for mobile, you might see a drop in rankings, even if your desktop version is perfect.

RankBrain is Google's AI system that helps process search results. It's a machine learning system that understands complex queries and improves the relevance of search results. RankBrain looks at various factors, such as the user's location, search history, and the context of the query, to deliver the best results. It's like a smart assistant that helps Google understand what you're looking for, even if you don't type in the exact keywords. This makes search results more accurate and helpful.

Page speed is a critical factor in Google's algorithm. Faster pages provide a better user experience and are more likely to rank higher. If your site takes too long to load, users might leave before it even finishes. Google uses various metrics to measure page speed, including time to first byte (TTFB), load time, and interactivity. Improving your page speed involves optimizing images, leveraging browser caching, and reducing server response times. A faster site not only improves your rankings but also keeps users happy.

Secure websites using HTTPS are favored by Google. HTTPS encrypts the data exchanged between your site and its users, making it more secure. Google considers site security a ranking factor because it wants to protect users from potential threats. Switching to HTTPS can improve your rankings and build trust with your audience. It's a win-win situation: better security and better search visibility. If your site is still on HTTP, it's time to make the switch to stay competitive.

User experience (UX) is a major factor in Google's algorithm. Good UX means users can easily navigate your site, find the information they need, and have a pleasant experience overall. Factors like site design, content layout, and ease of use all contribute to UX. Google measures UX using metrics such as bounce rate, time on site, and pages per session. A well-designed site with high-quality content and easy navigation will keep users engaged and improve your rankings.

Local SEO factors are important for businesses that serve specific geographic areas. Google uses signals like Google My Business listings, local citations, and reviews to determine local rankings. If you run a local business, optimizing your site for local search is crucial. This involves claiming and optimizing your Google My Business profile, getting listed in local directories, and encouraging customer reviews. Local SEO helps you reach potential customers in your area and improves your visibility in local search results.

Algorithm penalties can severely impact your rankings. Google penalizes sites that violate its guidelines, such as using black-hat SEO techniques or having low-quality content. Penalties can result in a significant drop in rankings or even removal from search results. Avoiding penalties involves following best practices, such as creating high-quality content, building ethical backlinks, and providing a good user experience. If your site is penalized, identifying and fixing the issues is crucial to recover your rankings.

Core Web Vitals are specific factors Google considers important for user experience. These include metrics like Largest Contentful Paint (LCP), First Input Delay (FID), and Cumulative Layout Shift (CLS). LCP measures how quickly the main content of a page loads, FID measures the time it takes for a page to become interactive, and CLS measures the stability of content as it loads. Optimizing these metrics can improve your site's performance and rankings.

Google's E-A-T principle stands for Expertise, Authoritativeness, and Trustworthiness. These factors are important for ranking, especially for content that impacts users' health, finances, or safety. Google wants to ensure the content it ranks is created by experts, is authoritative, and is trustworthy. Building E-A-T involves showcasing your expertise, gaining authority through backlinks and citations, and building trust with your audience through transparent and ethical practices.

Content freshness is another key factor in Google's algorithm. Fresh content is more likely to rank higher, especially for queries that require up-to-date information. Regularly updating your content with new information, latest trends, and current data can improve your rankings. This doesn't mean you need to update your entire site frequently, but keeping key pages and popular posts current can make a big difference. Fresh content signals to Google that your site is active and relevant.

Structured data and schema markup help Google understand the content on your site better. Using structured data, you can provide additional information about your content, such as product details, reviews, and events. This helps Google display rich snippets in search results, which can improve your click-through rates and visibility. Implementing schema markup involves adding specific code to your pages that tells Google what the content is about. It's a powerful way to enhance your search presence.

Social signals, such as likes, shares, and comments, can indirectly impact your rankings. While social signals are not direct ranking factors, they can increase your content's visibility and drive traffic to your site. This increased traffic can lead to more backlinks and engagement, which are important ranking factors. Integrating social media into your SEO strategy can help amplify your content and reach a wider audience. The more your content is shared, the more likely it is to attract attention and rank higher.

Duplicate content can confuse search engines and lead to lower rankings. When Google finds multiple pages with the same content, it has to decide which one to rank. This can dilute your rankings and reduce your visibility. Avoiding duplicate content involves creating original content and using canonical tags to tell Google which version of a page to consider the primary one. Regularly auditing your site for duplicate content and fixing any issues can help maintain your rankings.

The presence of ads on your site can impact your rankings, especially if they interfere with user experience. Google penalizes sites that have intrusive or excessive ads that make it difficult for users to find the content they're looking for. Ensuring your ads are placed in a way that doesn't disrupt the user experience is important. Ads should be relevant, non-intrusive, and not cover the main content. Balancing ads and content can help maintain a good user experience and rankings.

Personalization in search results means Google tailors the results based on individual user preferences and behavior. Factors like search history, location, and past interactions with your site influence how your content appears in search results. This personalization can make it challenging to rank consistently, as different users may see different results. Understanding how personalization works can help you create content that appeals to a broader audience while still targeting specific user needs.

There are many myths about Google's algorithm that can lead you astray. One common myth is that you need to constantly update your site to rank well. While fresh content is important, quality and relevance are more critical. Another myth is that using paid ads can boost your organic rankings. In reality, paid and organic search operate independently. It's important to focus on proven strategies and best practices rather than chasing myths that don't have any real impact on your rankings.

To sum up, understanding Google's algorithm is crucial for SEO success. By focusing on the key factors like keywords, user intent, backlinks, content quality, and user experience, you can improve your rankings and visibility. Staying updated with algorithm changes and adapting your strategy accordingly can help you stay ahead in the competitive world of SEO.

Chapter 2: Keyword Research Mastery

Keyword research is the foundation of any successful SEO strategy. It's like finding the right ingredients for a delicious recipe. By understanding which keywords people use to search for information, you can create content that meets their needs and ranks higher in search results. The first step in keyword research is understanding your audience. Knowing who they are, what they're looking for, and how they search for it is crucial. This helps you choose the right keywords that match their search intent.

Choosing the right keywords is like picking the best tools for a job. You need to find keywords that are relevant to your content and have a good balance of search volume and competition. High-volume keywords can drive more traffic, but they're also more competitive. On the other hand, low-volume keywords are easier to rank for but may not bring as much traffic. Finding the right balance is key to a successful keyword strategy. Using keyword research tools can help you identify these opportunities.

There are different types of keywords to consider. Short-tail keywords are broad and general, like "shoes," while long-tail keywords are more specific, like "running shoes for women." Long-tail keywords are usually less competitive and have a clearer search intent. They might not bring as much traffic as short-tail keywords, but the traffic they do bring is more targeted and likely to convert. Including a mix of both in your strategy can help you reach a wider audience.

Keyword research tools are essential for finding the right keywords. Tools like Google Keyword Planner, Ahrefs, and SEMrush provide valuable data on search volume, competition, and keyword suggestions.

These tools can help you identify keyword opportunities and understand how your competitors are performing. They also provide insights into trends and seasonal variations, which can help you plan your content strategy. Using these tools effectively can give you a competitive edge in keyword research.

Analyzing keyword difficulty is an important step in keyword research. Keyword difficulty measures how hard it is to rank for a particular keyword. High-difficulty keywords are more competitive and harder to rank for, while low-difficulty keywords are easier to rank for but may not bring as much traffic. Balancing difficulty and search volume is crucial for a successful keyword strategy. Tools like Moz and Ahrefs provide keyword difficulty scores that can help you make informed decisions.

Search volume indicates how many people are searching for a particular keyword. High search volume means more potential traffic, but it also means more competition. Understanding search volume helps you choose keywords that can bring significant traffic to your site. It's important to consider both monthly and seasonal search volumes, as some keywords may be popular only at certain times of the year. Analyzing search volume data helps you prioritize your keyword list and plan your content calendar.

Search intent is the reason behind a user's search query. Understanding search intent helps you create content that meets the user's needs and ranks higher in search results. There are different types of search intent: informational (looking for information), navigational (looking for a specific website), and transactional (looking to make a purchase). Matching your content to the user's search intent is crucial for SEO success. For example, a blog post might target informational intent, while a product page targets transactional intent.

Brainstorming keyword ideas is an important part of keyword research. Start by thinking about the topics and questions your audience is interested in. Use tools like Google Autocomplete, Answer the Public, and forums to find popular queries related to your niche. Analyzing competitor content can also provide valuable keyword ideas. Looking at what keywords your competitors are targeting can help you identify gaps and opportunities in your own strategy. The goal is to create a comprehensive list of keywords that are relevant and valuable.

Competitor analysis provides valuable insights into what keywords are working for other sites in your niche. By analyzing competitor keywords, you can identify opportunities to target similar keywords or find gaps where you can offer better content. Tools like Ahrefs and SEMrush allow you to see which keywords your competitors are ranking for and how they're performing. This information helps you refine your keyword strategy and stay competitive in your niche.

LSI (Latent Semantic Indexing) keywords are related terms that add context to your content. They help search engines understand the topic of your page and improve its relevance. Including LSI keywords in your content can enhance its SEO performance. These keywords are not necessarily synonyms, but they are related in meaning. For example, if your main keyword is "digital marketing," LSI keywords might include "online advertising," "SEO," and "social media marketing." Using LSI keywords naturally in your content can improve its relevance and ranking.

Creating a keyword list involves compiling all the keywords you've identified through research. This list should include a mix of short-tail and long-tail keywords, as well as primary and secondary keywords. Primary keywords are the main focus of your content, while secondary keywords support the main topic and add context. Organizing your keyword list helps you plan your content strategy and ensures you're targeting the right terms. Regularly updating this list based on performance and new research is essential for staying competitive.

Prioritizing keywords is crucial for effective SEO. Not all keywords are created equal, so you need to focus on the ones that offer the best opportunities. Consider factors like search volume, competition, and relevance to your content. Prioritizing helps you allocate your resources effectively and focus on keywords that can drive the most traffic and conversions. It's a strategic process that involves balancing short-term wins with long-term goals. By prioritizing keywords, you can create a roadmap for your content strategy and achieve better results.

Finding keyword gaps involves identifying keywords that your competitors are ranking for but you're not. These gaps represent opportunities to create content that can fill those voids and attract traffic. Tools like Ahrefs and SEMrush provide keyword gap analysis features that highlight these opportunities. Addressing keyword gaps helps you expand your reach and capture more search traffic. It's an ongoing process that requires regular analysis and adaptation. By filling keyword gaps, you can stay ahead of the competition and grow your organic traffic.

Long-tail keyword strategy focuses on targeting specific, less competitive keywords that have a clear search intent. These keywords may have lower search volumes, but they attract more targeted traffic. Long-tail keywords are often easier to rank for and can drive highly relevant visitors to your site. Creating content around long-tail keywords involves understanding your audience's needs and addressing them directly. This strategy can improve your overall SEO performance and help you reach niche markets. By focusing on long-tail keywords, you can build a strong foundation for your SEO efforts.

Local SEO involves targeting keywords specific to your geographic area. For businesses that serve a local market, local keywords are crucial for attracting nearby customers. These keywords often include location-specific terms, such as "best pizza in New York" or "plumber in Chicago." Optimizing your content for local keywords involves creating location-based pages, optimizing your Google My Business profile, and getting listed in local directories. Local SEO helps you reach potential customers in your area and improves your visibility in local search results.

Seasonal keyword trends are important to consider in your keyword strategy. Some keywords are popular only at certain times of the year, such as "Christmas gifts" or "summer vacation ideas." Analyzing seasonal trends helps you plan your content calendar and create timely content that matches these peaks in search interest. Tools like Google Trends provide insights into seasonal keyword patterns. By aligning your content strategy with seasonal trends, you can attract more traffic during peak times and stay relevant to your audience.

Tracking keyword performance is essential for measuring the success of your SEO efforts. Regularly monitoring your keyword rankings helps you understand what's working and what needs improvement. Tools like Google Search Console, Ahrefs, and SEMrush provide detailed reports on keyword performance, including rankings, traffic, and click-through rates. Analyzing this data helps you make informed decisions and adjust your strategy as needed. Continuous tracking and optimization are key to maintaining and improving your keyword rankings.

Integrating keywords into your content involves using them naturally and strategically. Keywords should be placed in key areas like the title, headings, meta descriptions, and throughout the body of the content. However, it's important to avoid keyword stuffing, which can lead to penalties. Instead, focus on creating high-quality content that addresses the user's needs and incorporates keywords seamlessly. The goal is to make your content relevant and valuable to both users and search engines.

Keyword stuffing is a practice to avoid in SEO. It involves overusing keywords in an attempt to manipulate search rankings. This tactic can lead to penalties from search engines and harm your site's reputation. Instead of stuffing keywords, focus on creating high-quality content that uses keywords naturally. This approach ensures your content is relevant and valuable to users, which ultimately leads to better rankings. Avoiding keyword stuffing helps maintain the integrity of your content and improves user experience.

Synonyms and variations are important in keyword integration. Using different forms of your main keywords helps avoid repetition and enhances your content's relevance. For example, if your main keyword is "running shoes," you can also use variations like "jogging shoes" or "athletic footwear." This approach provides a more comprehensive coverage of the topic and improves your chances of ranking for different search queries. Using synonyms and variations makes your content more engaging and helps it appeal to a broader audience.

Keyword cannibalization occurs when multiple pages on your site compete for the same keyword. This can dilute your rankings and confuse search engines about which page to prioritize. Avoiding keyword cannibalization involves creating distinct, focused content for each keyword. Using canonical tags and internal linking can also help manage this issue. Regularly auditing your site for keyword cannibalization ensures your pages are optimized effectively and don't compete against each other. Addressing this issue improves your overall SEO performance.

Using keywords in URLs and meta tags is a best practice in SEO. Including keywords in your page URLs, meta titles, and meta descriptions helps search engines understand the content of your pages.

This can improve your rankings and click-through rates. However, it's important to keep URLs and meta tags concise and relevant. Avoid keyword stuffing and focus on creating descriptive and informative tags that accurately represent your content. Properly optimized URLs and meta tags enhance your site's SEO and user experience.

Updating your keyword strategy over time is essential for staying competitive. As search trends and user behavior evolve, your keyword strategy should adapt accordingly. Regularly reviewing and updating your keyword list based on performance data helps you stay relevant and capture new opportunities. This involves analyzing search trends, competitor performance, and user feedback. Keeping your keyword strategy current ensures your content remains effective and continues to attract traffic. Adapting to changes in the SEO landscape is key to long-term success.

Case studies of successful keyword strategies provide valuable insights and inspiration. Analyzing how other sites have achieved success with their keyword research can help you refine your own approach. Look for case studies that highlight different aspects of keyword strategy, such as long-tail keywords, local SEO, or content optimization. Learning from real-world examples helps you understand best practices and avoid common pitfalls. Applying these lessons to your own strategy can improve your keyword research and overall SEO performance.

In summary, mastering keyword research is a fundamental step in achieving SEO success. By understanding your audience, choosing the right keywords, and using them effectively, you can create content that ranks well and attracts targeted traffic. Regularly updating your keyword strategy and tracking performance helps you stay competitive and adapt to changes in the search landscape. With the right approach to keyword research, you can build a strong foundation for your SEO efforts and achieve better results.

Chapter 3: Crafting High-Quality Content

High-quality content is the backbone of a successful SEO strategy. It's like building a house: without a strong foundation, everything else will crumble. High-quality content attracts visitors, keeps them engaged, and encourages them to return. It also helps you rank higher in search results because Google values content that provides value to users. Creating high-quality content starts with understanding your audience. Knowing what they're looking for and how they search for it helps you create content that meets their needs and interests.

Understanding your audience involves researching their demographics, interests, and behaviors. This helps you create content that resonates with them and addresses their pain points. For example, if your audience is interested in gardening, you can create detailed guides on different gardening techniques, plant care tips, and seasonal gardening tasks. By providing valuable and relevant information, you can build trust with your audience and keep them coming back for more. Knowing your audience also helps you choose the right keywords and topics for your content.

Defining your content goals is an essential step in creating high-quality content. Your goals might include increasing website traffic, generating leads, boosting engagement, or building brand awareness. Clearly defined goals help you stay focused and measure the success of your content. For example, if your goal is to increase traffic, you might create blog posts that target high-volume keywords and share them on social media. If your goal is to generate leads, you might create in-depth guides or eBooks that require users to provide their email addresses to access.

Brainstorming content ideas is a creative process that involves thinking about the topics and questions your audience is interested in. You can use tools like Google Trends, social media platforms, and forums to find popular topics in your niche. You can also analyze competitor content to see what's working for them and identify gaps in your own content. Creating a content calendar helps you plan your content strategy and ensure you're consistently publishing new and relevant content. Brainstorming and planning are key to maintaining a steady flow of high-quality content.

There are different types of content that rank well in search results. Blog posts, articles, infographics, videos, and podcasts are all effective content formats. Each format has its advantages and can help you reach a wider audience. For example, blog posts are great for providing detailed information and attracting organic traffic. Videos are engaging and can help you reach a broader audience on platforms like YouTube. Infographics are visually appealing and easy to share on social media. Using a mix of content formats helps you engage different segments of your audience.

Writing compelling headlines is crucial for attracting readers to your content. A good headline grabs attention, sparks curiosity, and encourages people to click. It should be clear, concise, and include your main keyword. Using numbers, questions, and power words can make your headlines more appealing. For example, a headline like "10 Easy Tips for Growing Tomatoes" is more engaging than "Tomato Growing Tips." Spending time crafting your headlines can significantly improve your content's click-through rate and overall performance.

Creating engaging introductions is important for keeping readers interested in your content. The introduction should hook your readers, provide a brief overview of what the content will cover, and encourage them to keep reading. You can use a compelling story, a surprising fact, or a thought-provoking question to grab attention. The introduction sets the tone for the rest of your content and helps establish a connection with your audience. A strong introduction can make the difference between a reader staying on your page or bouncing away.

Content structure is another important aspect of high-quality content. Organizing your content in a clear and logical manner makes it easier for readers to follow and understand. Using headings, subheadings, bullet points, and numbered lists can break up your content and make it more readable. Each section should flow naturally into the next, providing a seamless reading experience. A well-structured piece of content is not only easier to read but also more likely to rank higher in search results. Google favors content that is well-organized and easy to navigate.

Writing for readability involves using clear and simple language that is easy for readers to understand. Avoid using jargon or complex words that might confuse your audience. Instead, focus on using a conversational tone and short sentences. Break up long paragraphs into smaller chunks to make your content more digestible. Using images, charts, and other visuals can also enhance readability and make your content more engaging. Readability is crucial for keeping readers on your page and ensuring they absorb the information you're providing.

Visuals play a significant role in enhancing your content. Images, videos, infographics, and charts can make your content more appealing and easier to understand. Visuals can also help illustrate complex ideas and provide additional context. For example, a chart can help explain data trends, while an infographic can summarize a long article. Using high-quality visuals can improve user experience and keep readers engaged. Make sure to optimize your images for SEO by using descriptive filenames and alt text that include your keywords.

Multimedia content, such as videos and podcasts, can take your content to the next level. Videos are highly engaging and can help you reach a wider audience on platforms like YouTube and social media. They're also great for explaining complex topics and providing tutorials. Podcasts are another effective format for reaching your audience, especially those who prefer audio content. Including multimedia in your content strategy can enhance your reach and engagement. It also provides different ways for your audience to consume your content.

Using data and research in your content adds credibility and value. Including statistics, studies, and expert quotes can support your points and make your content more authoritative. Always cite your sources and provide links to the original research. This not only builds trust with your audience but also enhances your content's SEO. Google favors content that is well-researched and backed by credible sources. Using data and research helps you create high-quality content that stands out and provides real value to your readers.

Writing for user intent means creating content that meets the needs and expectations of your audience. Understanding user intent helps you tailor your content to what users are looking for. For example, if users are searching for "how to bake a cake," they likely want a step-by-step guide, not just general information about cakes. Matching your content to user intent improves its relevance and increases the chances of ranking higher in search results. Always keep your audience's needs in mind when creating content.

Original content is crucial for SEO success. Google favors unique and original content over duplicate or copied content. Creating original content involves offering new insights, perspectives, and information that can't be found elsewhere. This not only helps you rank higher but also builds your authority and credibility. Avoiding plagiarism and citing your sources properly is essential. Original content provides value to your audience and sets you apart from your competitors. It's the foundation of a strong SEO strategy.

Duplicate content issues can negatively impact your SEO. When Google finds multiple pages with the same content, it has to decide which one to rank. This can dilute your rankings and reduce your visibility. Avoiding duplicate content involves creating original content and using canonical tags to indicate the primary version of a page. Regularly auditing your site for duplicate content and fixing any issues can help maintain your rankings. Ensuring your content is unique and original is key to SEO success.

Updating and refreshing your content is important for maintaining its relevance and effectiveness. Over time, information can become outdated, and new trends can emerge. Regularly reviewing and updating your content helps ensure it stays current and valuable to your audience. This can involve adding new information, updating statistics, and improving readability. Keeping your content fresh signals to Google that your site is active and relevant. Regular updates can improve your rankings and keep your audience engaged.

Evergreen content is content that remains relevant and valuable over time. Unlike seasonal or trend-based content, evergreen content addresses timeless topics that continue to attract traffic long after it's published. Examples include how-to guides, tutorials, and FAQs. Creating evergreen content is a smart strategy for long-term SEO success. It provides ongoing value to your audience and continues to drive traffic to your site. By focusing on evergreen topics, you can build a strong foundation of high-quality content that stands the test of time.

Storytelling is a powerful tool in content creation. Telling a compelling story can engage your audience, evoke emotions, and make your content more memorable. Stories help illustrate your points and make complex ideas easier to understand. They also create a connection with your audience, making them more likely to stay on your page and return for more. Incorporating storytelling into your content can enhance its impact and effectiveness. Whether it's a personal anecdote or a case study, stories can bring your content to life.

Actionable content provides practical tips and advice that readers can apply immediately. It goes beyond theory and offers concrete steps that help solve a problem or achieve a goal. Actionable content is highly valuable to readers and can drive more engagement and conversions. For example, a blog post that offers step-by-step instructions for a DIY project or a checklist for improving productivity provides real value. Creating actionable content helps you build trust with your audience and establish yourself as an authority in your niche.

Content formatting plays a crucial role in readability and user experience. Proper formatting involves using headings, subheadings, bullet points, and numbered lists to organize your content. This makes it easier for readers to scan and find the information they need. Formatting also includes using short paragraphs, bold text, and images to break up the content and make it more visually appealing. Well-formatted content improves readability and keeps readers engaged. It also signals to Google that your content is well-structured and user-friendly.

Internal linking is an effective SEO strategy that involves linking to other pages on your site. Internal links help users navigate your site and find related content. They also help search engines understand the structure of your site and discover new pages. Using internal links strategically can improve your site's SEO and keep readers on your site longer. Linking to relevant content provides additional value to your audience and enhances their experience. It's a simple but powerful way to boost your SEO and engagement.

Writing meta descriptions and titles is an important part of on-page SEO. Meta titles and descriptions provide a brief summary of your content and appear in search results. They should be concise, descriptive, and include your main keyword. A compelling meta description can improve your click-through rate and drive more traffic to your site. Crafting effective meta titles and descriptions involves balancing SEO with user experience. They should accurately represent your content and entice users to click.

Examples of high-quality content can provide inspiration and insights into what works well. Analyzing successful content in your niche helps you understand best practices and identify opportunities for improvement. Look for content that is well-researched, engaging, and provides real value to readers. Studying examples of high-quality content helps you refine your own content strategy and create better content. Learning from the success of others can help you avoid common pitfalls and achieve better results.

To sum up, crafting high-quality content is essential for SEO success. By understanding your audience, defining your goals, and using the right strategies, you can create content that ranks well and provides value to your readers. High-quality content attracts traffic, engages your audience, and builds your authority. It's the foundation of a strong SEO strategy and the key to long-term success.

Chapter 4: On-Page SEO Techniques

On-page SEO involves optimizing individual web pages to rank higher and attract more traffic from search engines. It's like decorating a house to make it more appealing to visitors. On-page SEO includes various elements such as title tags, meta descriptions, header tags, and content optimization. Each element plays a crucial role in improving your site's visibility and relevance. By optimizing these elements, you can enhance your site's SEO performance and provide a better user experience.

Title tags are one of the most important on-page SEO elements. The title tag appears in search results and tells both users and search engines what your page is about. It should be concise, descriptive, and include your main keyword. A well-crafted title tag can improve your click-through rate and help your page rank higher. It's important to keep title tags under 60 characters to ensure they don't get cut off in search results. Using compelling language and power words can make your title tags more attractive to users.

Meta descriptions provide a brief summary of your page's content and appear below the title tag in search results. They should be clear, concise, and include your main keyword. A compelling meta description can improve your click-through rate and drive more traffic to your site. It should provide enough information to entice users to click while accurately representing your content. Meta descriptions should be around 150-160 characters to ensure they're fully displayed in search results. Crafting effective meta descriptions involves balancing SEO with user experience.

Header tags (H1, H2, H3, etc.) are used to structure your content and make it more readable. The H1 tag is the main heading of your page and should include your primary keyword. Subheadings (H2, H3, etc.) help organize your content and break it up into sections. Using header tags properly can improve your content's readability and SEO. They help search engines understand the structure and hierarchy of your content. Including keywords in your header tags can enhance your page's relevance and ranking.

Optimizing images is an important aspect of on-page SEO. Images can enhance your content and make it more engaging, but they need to be properly optimized. This involves using descriptive filenames and alt text that include your keywords. Alt text helps search engines understand what an image is about and improves accessibility for users with visual impairments. Compressing images to reduce file size can improve page load times, which is a ranking factor. Using high-quality images that are relevant to your content can enhance user experience and SEO.

Alt text is a description of an image that helps search engines understand its content. It also improves accessibility by providing a text alternative for users who can't see the image. Including keywords in your alt text can enhance your on-page SEO. However, it's important to use descriptive and accurate alt text that accurately represents the image. Avoid keyword stuffing and focus on providing useful information. Properly optimized alt text can improve your image search rankings and overall SEO.

URL structure plays a crucial role in on-page SEO. Clean and descriptive URLs that include your main keyword can improve your rankings and click-through rates. URLs should be concise, easy to read, and accurately reflect the content of the page. Using hyphens to separate words and avoiding special characters can make your URLs more user-friendly. Consistent URL structure across your site helps search engines understand your site's organization and improve crawlability. Optimizing your URLs is a simple but effective way to boost your on-page SEO.

Internal linking involves linking to other pages on your site. It helps users navigate your site and find related content. Internal links also help search engines understand the structure of your site and discover new pages. Using internal links strategically can improve your site's SEO and keep readers on your site longer. Linking to relevant content provides additional value to your audience and enhances their experience. It's a simple but powerful way to boost your SEO and engagement.

Creating an SEO-friendly sitemap helps search engines index your site more efficiently. A sitemap is a file that lists all the pages on your site and provides information about their relationships and updates. Submitting your sitemap to Google Search Console can help ensure your site is crawled and indexed properly. An XML sitemap is the most common format and is supported by all major search engines. Keeping your sitemap up-to-date is important for maintaining your site's SEO. An SEO-friendly sitemap improves your site's visibility and crawlability.

Content plays a crucial role in on-page SEO. High-quality, relevant content that provides value to users is essential for ranking well. Your content should be well-written, informative, and optimized for your target keywords. Including keywords naturally throughout your content helps search engines understand its relevance. However, avoid keyword stuffing and focus on creating content that meets user needs. Regularly updating and refreshing your content can also improve your rankings. Quality content is the foundation of a strong on-page SEO strategy.

Schema markup helps search engines understand the content on your site better. Using schema markup, you can provide additional information about your content, such as product details, reviews, and events. This helps search engines display rich snippets in search results, which can improve your click-through rates and visibility. Implementing schema markup involves adding specific code to your pages that tells search engines what the content is about. It's a powerful way to enhance your search presence and provide more detailed information to users.

Mobile optimization is essential for on-page SEO. With more people using smartphones to browse the web, your site needs to be mobile-friendly to rank well. Responsive design, fast loading times, and easy navigation are key factors. Ensuring your content is readable on small screens and providing a seamless mobile experience can improve your rankings. Google uses mobile-first indexing, which means it primarily uses the mobile version of your site for ranking and indexing. Optimizing your site for mobile is crucial for staying competitive in search results.

Improving page speed is important for both user experience and SEO. Faster pages provide a better user experience and are more likely to rank higher. If your site takes too long to load, users might leave before it even finishes. Google uses various metrics to measure page speed, including time to first byte (TTFB), load time, and interactivity. Improving your page speed involves optimizing images, leveraging browser caching, and reducing server response times. A faster site not only improves your rankings but also keeps users happy.

User experience (UX) is a major factor in on-page SEO. Good UX means users can easily navigate your site, find the information they need, and have a pleasant experience overall. Factors like site design, content layout, and ease of use all contribute to UX. Google measures UX using metrics such as bounce rate, time on site, and pages per session. A well-designed site with high-quality content and easy navigation will keep users engaged and improve your rankings.

Duplicate content issues can negatively impact your SEO. When Google finds multiple pages with the same content, it has to decide which one to rank. This can dilute your rankings and reduce your visibility. Avoiding duplicate content involves creating original content and using canonical tags to indicate the primary version of a page. Regularly auditing your site for duplicate content and fixing any issues can help maintain your rankings. Ensuring your content is unique and original is key to SEO success.

Canonical tags help prevent duplicate content issues by indicating the primary version of a page. When you have multiple pages with similar content, using canonical tags tells search engines which version to consider the main one. This helps consolidate link equity and improve your rankings. Implementing canonical tags is a simple but effective way to manage duplicate content and maintain your site's SEO. Properly using canonical tags ensures your content is correctly indexed and ranked by search engines.

Local SEO involves optimizing your site for local search queries. This is important for businesses that serve specific geographic areas. Google uses signals like Google My Business listings, local citations, and reviews to determine local rankings. Optimizing your site for local SEO involves creating location-based pages, optimizing your Google My Business profile, and getting listed in local directories. Local SEO helps you reach potential customers in your area and improves your visibility in local search results.

HTTPS is a ranking factor in Google's algorithm. It encrypts the data exchanged between your site and its users, making it more secure. Switching to HTTPS can improve your rankings and build trust with your audience. Sites that use HTTP are marked as "Not Secure" in browsers, which can deter users. Migrating to HTTPS involves obtaining an SSL certificate and updating your site's URLs. Ensuring your site is secure with HTTPS is essential for both SEO and user trust.

Social sharing buttons can enhance your on-page SEO by making it easy for users to share your content on social media. Social signals, such as likes, shares, and comments, can indirectly impact your rankings. While social signals are not direct ranking factors, they can increase your content's visibility and drive traffic to your site. Integrating social sharing buttons into your site can help amplify your content and reach a wider audience. The more your content is shared, the more likely it is to attract attention and rank higher.

Outbound links to reputable sources can improve your content's credibility and relevance. Linking to high-quality, authoritative sites shows search engines that your content is well-researched and trustworthy. Outbound links can also provide additional value to your readers by directing them to useful resources. However, it's important to use outbound links sparingly and ensure they're relevant to your content. Properly using outbound links can enhance your site's SEO and user experience.

Avoiding on-page SEO mistakes is crucial for maintaining your rankings. Common mistakes include keyword stuffing, duplicate content, slow page speed, and poor mobile optimization. Regularly auditing your site and fixing any issues can help maintain your rankings. Staying updated with best practices and algorithm changes is also important. By avoiding common mistakes and following best practices, you can enhance your on-page SEO and improve your site's visibility.

Using analytics for on-page SEO helps you measure the effectiveness of your optimization efforts. Tools like Google Analytics and Google Search Console provide valuable data on site performance, user behavior, and keyword rankings. Analyzing this data helps you identify areas for improvement and adjust your strategy as needed. Regularly monitoring your site's performance ensures you stay on track and make informed decisions. Using analytics is essential for maintaining and improving your on-page SEO.

Case studies of successful on-page SEO provide valuable insights and inspiration. Analyzing how other sites have achieved success with their on-page optimization can help you refine your own strategy. Look for case studies that highlight different aspects of on-page SEO, such as content optimization, mobile optimization, or site speed improvements. Learning from real-world examples helps you understand best practices and avoid common pitfalls. Applying these lessons to your own strategy can improve your on-page SEO and overall performance.

Regularly auditing your on-page SEO is important for maintaining your rankings. An SEO audit involves reviewing all aspects of your on-page optimization, including content, technical elements, and user experience. Identifying and fixing any issues can help improve your rankings and site performance. Regular audits ensure your site stays up-to-date with best practices and algorithm changes. By regularly auditing your on-page SEO, you can maintain your rankings and provide a better user experience.

To sum up, on-page SEO involves optimizing various elements of your web pages to improve their visibility and relevance. By focusing on key elements like title tags, meta descriptions, header tags, content optimization, and site structure, you can enhance your on-page SEO and provide a better user experience. Regularly auditing and updating your on-page optimization ensures your site stays competitive and ranks well in search results.

Chapter 5: Technical SEO Fundamentals

Technical SEO involves optimizing your website's infrastructure to improve its visibility and performance in search engines. It's like ensuring the foundation of your house is solid and well-built. Technical SEO includes elements such as site speed, mobile optimization, site architecture, and crawlability. By optimizing these technical aspects, you can enhance your site's SEO performance and provide a better user experience.

Website architecture plays a crucial role in technical SEO. A well-structured site is easy for users to navigate and for search engines to crawl. Organizing your content into clear categories and using a logical hierarchy helps search engines understand your site's structure. Using a flat architecture, where important pages are only a few clicks away from the homepage, can improve crawlability and rankings. A well-organized site structure enhances user experience and helps search engines index your content more efficiently.

Improving site speed is essential for both user experience and SEO. Faster sites provide a better user experience and are more likely to rank higher. Google uses various metrics to measure site speed, including time to first byte (TTFB), load time, and interactivity. Improving your site speed involves optimizing images, leveraging browser caching, and reducing server response times. A faster site not only improves your rankings but also keeps users happy. Tools like Google PageSpeed Insights can help you identify areas for improvement.

Mobile-friendliness is a critical factor in technical SEO. With more people using smartphones to browse the web, your site needs to be optimized for mobile devices. Responsive design, fast loading times, and easy navigation are key factors. Ensuring your content is readable on small screens and providing a seamless mobile experience can improve your rankings. Google uses mobile-first indexing, which means it primarily uses the mobile version of your site for ranking and indexing. Optimizing your site for mobile is crucial for staying competitive in search results.

Robots.txt is a file that tells search engines which pages on your site to crawl and which to avoid. Properly configuring your robots.txt file can help ensure search engines index your important pages while avoiding duplicate or low-quality content. This file should be placed in the root directory of your site and follow the standard format. Incorrectly configuring your robots.txt file can prevent search engines from crawling your site, so it's important to get it right. Regularly reviewing and updating your robots.txt file can help maintain your site's SEO.

An XML sitemap is a file that lists all the pages on your site and provides information about their relationships and updates. Submitting your sitemap to Google Search Console can help ensure your site is crawled and indexed properly. An XML sitemap is the most common format and is supported by all major search engines. Keeping your sitemap up-to-date is important for maintaining your site's SEO. An SEO-friendly sitemap improves your site's visibility and crawlability. It's a powerful tool for ensuring your content is indexed and ranked by search engines.

Handling 404 errors is important for maintaining your site's SEO and user experience. A 404 error occurs when a page can't be found, which can frustrate users and hurt your rankings. Setting up custom 404 pages that provide helpful information and redirect users to relevant content can improve user experience. Regularly monitoring your site for broken links and fixing any issues can help maintain your rankings. Ensuring your site is free of 404 errors provides a better experience for users and search engines.

HTTPS is a ranking factor in Google's algorithm. It encrypts the data exchanged between your site and its users, making it more secure. Switching to HTTPS can improve your rankings and build trust with your audience. Sites that use HTTP are marked as "Not Secure" in browsers, which can deter users. Migrating to HTTPS involves obtaining an SSL certificate and updating your site's URLs. Ensuring your site is secure with HTTPS is essential for both SEO and user trust. A secure site provides a better experience for users and enhances your search visibility.

Canonical tags help prevent duplicate content issues by indicating the primary version of a page. When you have multiple pages with similar content, using canonical tags tells search engines which version to consider the main one. This helps consolidate link equity and improve your rankings. Implementing canonical tags is a simple but effective way to manage duplicate content and maintain your site's SEO. Properly using canonical tags ensures your content is correctly indexed and ranked by search engines.

Crawl budget refers to the number of pages a search engine crawls on your site during a given time period. Optimizing your crawl budget helps ensure search engines prioritize your most important pages. This involves improving site speed, fixing broken links, and avoiding duplicate content. Tools like Google Search Console can help you monitor your crawl budget and identify areas for improvement. Efficiently managing your crawl budget ensures your content is indexed and ranked effectively.

Structured data, or schema markup, helps search engines understand the content on your site better. Using structured data, you can provide additional information about your content, such as product details, reviews, and events. This helps search engines display rich snippets in search results, which can improve your click-through rates and visibility. Implementing structured data involves adding specific code to your pages that tells search engines what the content is about. It's a powerful way to enhance your search presence and provide more detailed information to users.

Broken links can negatively impact your site's SEO and user experience. When users encounter broken links, it can frustrate them and lead to a higher bounce rate. Regularly monitoring your site for broken links and fixing any issues can help maintain your rankings. Tools like Google Search Console and Ahrefs can help you identify broken links on your site. Ensuring your site is free of broken links provides a better experience for users and enhances your search visibility.

Redirects are used to send users and search engines from one URL to another. They're important for maintaining your site's SEO when you change URLs or move content. There are different types of redirects, such as 301 (permanent) and 302 (temporary). Using the correct type of redirect ensures search engines understand your intentions and pass link equity to the new URL. Properly setting up redirects helps maintain your rankings and provides a seamless experience for users.

Site security is a critical factor in technical SEO. Ensuring your site is secure protects it from threats and builds trust with your audience. Using HTTPS, regularly updating your software, and implementing security measures like firewalls and malware scans can enhance your site's security. Google favors secure sites in its rankings, so maintaining a secure site is essential for SEO success. Regularly monitoring your site for security issues and addressing any vulnerabilities can help protect your site and maintain your rankings.

Server response time is the amount of time it takes for your server to respond to a request from a user's browser. Faster server response times provide a better user experience and can improve your rankings. Optimizing your server response time involves using a reliable hosting provider, optimizing your database, and reducing server load. Tools like Google PageSpeed Insights can help you identify areas for improvement. Ensuring your server responds quickly is essential for maintaining your site's SEO and user experience.

Browser caching helps reduce page load times by storing static files in the user's browser. This means the browser doesn't have to download these files each time the user visits your site. Leveraging browser caching can improve your site's speed and provide a better user experience. It involves configuring your server to specify how long browsers should cache files. Tools like Google PageSpeed Insights can help you set up browser caching. Faster page load times can improve your rankings and keep users on your site longer.

International SEO involves optimizing your site for different languages and regions. This is important if you have a global audience or operate in multiple countries. Using hreflang tags, creating localized content, and optimizing for local search engines can enhance your international SEO. Hreflang tags tell search engines which language and region a page is intended for, helping them deliver the right content to users. Properly implementing international SEO can improve your site's visibility and reach a broader audience.

Hreflang tags help search engines understand the language and regional targeting of your pages. They're essential for sites that offer content in multiple languages or target users in different regions. Using hreflang tags ensures search engines deliver the correct version of your content to users. Implementing hreflang tags involves adding specific code to your pages that indicates the language and region. Properly using hreflang tags can improve your international SEO and provide a better experience for users.

Clean code is important for maintaining your site's SEO and performance. Well-written, efficient code ensures your site loads quickly and functions properly. It also makes it easier for search engines to crawl and index your content. Regularly reviewing and optimizing your code can help improve your site's speed and SEO. This involves minimizing CSS and JavaScript files, removing unnecessary code, and using best practices for web development. Clean code enhances your site's user experience and search visibility.

Google Search Console is a valuable tool for monitoring and improving your site's SEO. It provides insights into your site's performance, search traffic, and indexing status. Using Google Search Console, you can identify and fix issues, submit sitemaps, and track keyword rankings. Regularly reviewing your Google Search Console data helps you make informed decisions and optimize your site's SEO. It's an essential tool for maintaining and improving your site's search visibility.

Common technical SEO issues include slow site speed, duplicate content, broken links, and poor mobile optimization. Regularly auditing your site and fixing any issues can help maintain your rankings. Staying updated with best practices and algorithm changes is also important. By addressing common technical SEO issues and following best practices, you can enhance your site's SEO and provide a better user experience.

AMP (Accelerated Mobile Pages) is a framework that helps create fast-loading mobile pages. Implementing AMP can improve your site's mobile performance and rankings. AMP pages are lightweight and designed to load quickly on mobile devices. Using AMP involves creating a separate version of your content with specific HTML, CSS, and JavaScript. Implementing AMP can enhance your mobile SEO and provide a better experience for users. Faster mobile pages can improve your rankings and keep users engaged.

Case studies of technical SEO improvements provide valuable insights and inspiration. Analyzing how other sites have achieved success with their technical optimization can help you refine your own strategy. Look for case studies that highlight different aspects of technical SEO, such as site speed improvements, mobile optimization, or site architecture enhancements. Learning from real-world examples helps you understand best practices and avoid common pitfalls. Applying these lessons to your own strategy can improve your technical SEO and overall performance.

To sum up, technical SEO involves optimizing your website's infrastructure to improve its visibility and performance in search engines. By focusing on key elements like site speed, mobile optimization, site architecture, and crawlability, you can enhance your technical SEO and provide a better user experience. Regularly auditing and updating your technical optimization ensures your site stays competitive and ranks well in search results.

Chapter 6: Building Quality Backlinks

Building quality backlinks is a crucial aspect of SEO. Backlinks are like votes of confidence for your website. When other sites link to yours, it signals to Google that your content is valuable and trustworthy. Not all backlinks are created equal, though. Links from reputable sites carry more weight than those from unknown or spammy sites. Building a strong backlink profile can significantly boost your rankings. But remember, it's about quality, not quantity. A few links from authoritative sites are better than many from low-quality ones.

Earning high-quality backlinks involves creating valuable and shareable content. Content that provides unique insights, in-depth information, or actionable tips is more likely to attract backlinks. Creating content that solves a problem, answers a question, or provides valuable information can encourage other sites to link to it. High-quality content acts as a magnet for backlinks and enhances your site's credibility. Investing time and effort in creating top-notch content is key to earning valuable backlinks.

Guest blogging is an effective strategy for building backlinks. It involves writing articles for other blogs in your niche and including links back to your site. Guest blogging helps you reach a wider audience, build relationships with other bloggers, and earn high-quality backlinks. To get started, identify reputable blogs in your niche and pitch them relevant and valuable content ideas. Writing high-quality guest posts can help you establish authority in your niche and attract more backlinks to your site.

Content marketing is another powerful way to build backlinks. Creating valuable, informative, and shareable content can attract links from other sites. This includes blog posts, infographics, videos, and eBooks. Promoting your content through social media, email marketing, and outreach can increase its visibility and attract more backlinks. By consistently producing high-quality content and promoting it effectively, you can build a strong backlink profile and improve your SEO.

Social media can help you build backlinks by increasing the visibility of your content. Sharing your content on social media platforms can attract attention and encourage others to link to it. Engaging with your audience and building a strong social media presence can enhance your content's reach and attract more backlinks. Using social media to promote your content and connect with influencers can amplify your backlink-building efforts. The more your content is shared, the more likely it is to attract backlinks.

Local backlinks are important for businesses that serve specific geographic areas. Getting links from local websites, directories, and industry associations can enhance your local SEO. Local backlinks signal to Google that your site is relevant to users in your area. Optimizing your Google My Business profile and getting listed in local directories can help you earn more local backlinks. Building relationships with local businesses and organizations can also provide opportunities for earning valuable local backlinks.

Industry directories can provide valuable backlinks to your site. Getting listed in reputable directories related to your niche can improve your site's visibility and credibility. These directories often have high domain authority, which can boost your rankings. Submitting your site to relevant directories and ensuring your information is accurate can help you earn quality backlinks. It's important to choose reputable directories and avoid spammy or low-quality ones.

Press releases can help you earn backlinks from news sites and industry publications. Writing and distributing press releases about significant events, product launches, or company news can attract media coverage and backlinks. Using press release distribution services can increase the reach of your releases and attract more backlinks. Crafting compelling and newsworthy press releases can enhance your backlink-building efforts and improve your site's SEO. Press releases provide an effective way to share your news and earn valuable backlinks.

Influencer outreach involves connecting with influencers in your niche and encouraging them to share or link to your content. Influencers have a large following and can amplify your content's reach. Building relationships with influencers through social media, email, and networking can help you earn backlinks from their websites and social profiles. Offering valuable content, collaborating on projects, or providing exclusive insights can incentivize influencers to link to your site. Influencer outreach is a powerful strategy for building backlinks and increasing your content's visibility.

Broken link building involves finding broken links on other websites and offering your content as a replacement. This strategy helps site owners fix broken links and provides you with valuable backlinks. Using tools like Ahrefs or Check My Links, you can identify broken links on relevant sites and reach out to the site owners with your replacement content. This approach not only helps you earn backlinks but also provides value to other site owners. Broken link building is an effective and mutually beneficial strategy for improving your backlink profile.

Internal linking is an effective SEO strategy that involves linking to other pages on your site. Internal links help users navigate your site and find related content. They also help search engines understand the structure of your site and discover new pages. Using internal links strategically can improve your site's SEO and keep readers on your site longer. Linking to relevant content provides additional value to your audience and enhances their experience. It's a simple but powerful way to boost your SEO and engagement.

Anchor text is the clickable text in a hyperlink. Using relevant and descriptive anchor text for your backlinks helps search engines understand the content of the linked page. It's important to use varied and natural anchor text to avoid over-optimization and penalties. Including keywords in your anchor text can enhance your page's relevance and ranking. Properly optimized anchor text improves the SEO value of your backlinks and provides a better user experience.

Disavowing bad backlinks is important for maintaining a healthy backlink profile. Low-quality or spammy backlinks can harm your rankings and credibility. Using tools like Google Search Console, you can identify and disavow bad backlinks to prevent them from affecting your site. Regularly monitoring your backlink profile and disavowing harmful links helps maintain your site's SEO and reputation. Ensuring your backlinks are from reputable and relevant sources is key to a strong backlink profile.

Understanding link penalties is crucial for avoiding and recovering from them. Google penalizes sites that engage in manipulative or unethical backlink practices, such as buying links or participating in link schemes. Penalties can result in a significant drop in rankings or even removal from search results. Following best practices and building ethical backlinks helps you avoid penalties. If your site is penalized, identifying and fixing the issues is crucial to recover your rankings. Ensuring your backlink strategy is ethical and compliant with Google's guidelines is essential for long-term SEO success.

Monitoring your backlink profile helps you understand the quality and impact of your backlinks. Regularly reviewing your backlinks using tools like Ahrefs, Moz, or Google Search Console can help you identify opportunities and address issues. Monitoring your backlink profile allows you to track the performance of your backlinks and make informed decisions. Regular analysis and adjustments ensure your backlink strategy remains effective and aligned with your SEO goals.

Case studies of successful backlink strategies provide valuable insights and inspiration. Analyzing how other sites have achieved success with their backlink-building efforts can help you refine your own strategy. Look for case studies that highlight different aspects of backlink building, such as content marketing, influencer outreach, or guest blogging. Learning from real-world examples helps you understand best practices and avoid common pitfalls. Applying these lessons to your own strategy can improve your backlink-building efforts and overall SEO performance.

Avoiding black hat SEO techniques is crucial for maintaining a healthy backlink profile. Black hat techniques, such as buying links or using link farms, can result in penalties and harm your rankings. Instead, focus on building ethical and high-quality backlinks through content marketing, guest blogging, and outreach. Following best practices and avoiding shortcuts ensures your backlink strategy is sustainable and effective. Ethical backlink building helps maintain your site's credibility and long-term SEO success.

Using tools to find backlink opportunities can enhance your backlink-building efforts. Tools like Ahrefs, SEMrush, and Moz provide valuable insights into your competitors' backlinks and help you identify new opportunities. These tools allow you to analyze backlink profiles, track performance, and discover potential link-building prospects. Using tools effectively can streamline your backlink-building process and improve your results. Leveraging technology and data can give you a competitive edge in building a strong backlink profile.

Link diversity is important for a healthy backlink profile. Having a variety of backlinks from different sources, such as blogs, news sites, directories, and social media, signals to Google that your site is valuable and credible. Relying too much on one type of backlink can make your profile look unnatural and risk penalties. Building diverse backlinks helps create a balanced and robust backlink profile. Ensuring your backlinks come from a wide range of reputable sources enhances your SEO and credibility.

Recovering from a link penalty involves identifying and fixing the issues that led to the penalty. This may involve disavowing bad backlinks, removing spammy links, and improving your overall backlink strategy. Using tools like Google Search Console and conducting a thorough backlink audit can help you identify the problematic links. Once you've addressed the issues, you can submit a reconsideration request to Google. Recovering from a link penalty requires effort and time, but it's essential for restoring your rankings and credibility.

The future of backlinks in SEO is evolving with changes in search algorithms and user behavior. While backlinks remain a crucial ranking factor, the focus is shifting towards quality and relevance. Building relationships, creating valuable content, and providing real value are key to earning backlinks in the future. Staying updated with industry trends and best practices helps you adapt to changes and maintain a strong backlink profile. The future of backlinks involves a more holistic and ethical approach to link building.

To sum up, building quality backlinks is essential for SEO success. By focusing on creating valuable content, engaging in ethical practices, and using effective strategies, you can build a strong backlink profile that enhances your rankings and credibility. Regularly monitoring and adjusting your backlink strategy ensures it remains effective and aligned with your SEO goals. A robust backlink profile is a key component of a successful SEO strategy and long-term online success.

Chapter 7: Local SEO Strategies

Local SEO involves optimizing your website and online presence to attract more business from relevant local searches. It's like putting up a big, bright sign in your neighborhood to let people know you're there. Local SEO is crucial for businesses that serve specific geographic areas, such as restaurants, retail stores, and service providers. By optimizing your site for local search, you can attract more customers from your area and improve your visibility in local search results.

Google My Business (GMB) is a critical component of local SEO. GMB is a free tool that allows businesses to manage their online presence on Google, including Search and Maps. Optimizing your GMB profile involves providing accurate and detailed information about your business, such as your address, phone number, hours of operation, and services. Encouraging customers to leave reviews and responding to them can also enhance your GMB profile. A well-optimized GMB profile can improve your local search visibility and attract more customers.

Local keywords are essential for local SEO. These are keywords that include location-specific terms, such as "best pizza in New York" or "plumber in Chicago." Using local keywords in your content, meta tags, and GMB profile can help you rank higher for local searches. Conducting keyword research to identify the most relevant and popular local keywords for your business is crucial. By targeting local keywords, you can attract more traffic from your area and improve your local SEO.

Backlinks from local websites, directories, and industry associations can enhance your local SEO. Local backlinks signal to Google that your site is relevant to users in your area. Getting listed in local directories and building relationships with local businesses can provide valuable backlink opportunities. Participating in local events and sponsorships can also help you earn local backlinks. Local backlinks are an important part of a strong local SEO strategy and can improve your visibility in local search results.

Online reviews play a significant role in local SEO. Positive reviews from satisfied customers can enhance your reputation and improve your local search rankings. Encouraging customers to leave reviews and responding to them promptly can build trust and credibility. Google considers reviews as a ranking factor for local search, so having a high volume of positive reviews can boost your local SEO. Managing your online reviews effectively is essential for attracting more customers and improving your local search visibility.

Local citations are mentions of your business's name, address, and phone number (NAP) on other websites. Consistent and accurate NAP information across the web helps Google verify your business's legitimacy and improve your local search rankings. Getting listed in reputable local directories, industry-specific websites, and local blogs can enhance your local SEO. Regularly auditing your citations to ensure consistency and accuracy is important. Local citations are a key component of a successful local SEO strategy.

NAP consistency is crucial for local SEO. Inconsistent or incorrect NAP information can confuse search engines and users, hurting your local search rankings. Ensuring your business's name, address, and phone number are consistent across all online platforms, including your website, GMB profile, and local citations, is essential. Regularly checking and updating your NAP information helps maintain consistency and improve your local SEO. Accurate NAP information builds trust with both search engines and users.

Optimizing your content for local search intent is important for attracting local customers. Local search intent involves queries with a local focus, such as "restaurants near me" or "best coffee shop in [city]." Creating content that addresses local search intent, such as local guides, event announcements, and community news, can improve your local SEO. Including local keywords and providing valuable information about your area can attract more local traffic. Understanding and addressing local search intent is key to a successful local SEO strategy.

Creating local content helps you connect with your community and improve your local SEO. Local content can include blog posts about local events, guides to your city, and stories about your business's involvement in the community. This type of content not only attracts local traffic but also builds relationships with local customers. Engaging with your community through local content enhances your local presence and improves your local search visibility. Local content is a valuable part of a strong local SEO strategy.

Social media can enhance your local SEO by increasing your visibility and engagement with your local audience. Sharing local content, promoting events, and engaging with your followers on social media platforms can boost your local presence. Encouraging customers to check in at your business and leave reviews on social media can also improve your local SEO. Building a strong social media presence and connecting with your local audience can enhance your local SEO and attract more customers.

Local directories provide valuable backlinks and citations that can improve your local SEO. Getting listed in reputable local directories, such as Yelp, Yellow Pages, and industry-specific directories, can enhance your visibility and credibility. Ensuring your NAP information is accurate and consistent across all directories is important. Submitting your business to relevant local directories can help you earn valuable backlinks and improve your local search rankings. Local directories are an essential part of a strong local SEO strategy.

Schema markup can help improve your local SEO by providing additional information about your business to search engines. Using local business schema, you can provide details such as your business's address, phone number, hours of operation, and services. This helps search engines display rich snippets in search results, which can improve your click-through rates and visibility. Implementing schema markup involves adding specific code to your pages that tells search engines what the content is about. Local schema markup enhances your local SEO and provides more detailed information to users.

Mobile optimization is crucial for local SEO. Many local searches are performed on mobile devices, so ensuring your site is mobile-friendly is essential. Responsive design, fast loading times, and easy navigation are key factors. Ensuring your content is readable on small screens and providing a seamless mobile experience can improve your local search rankings. Google uses mobile-first indexing, which means it primarily uses the mobile version of your site for ranking and indexing. Optimizing your site for mobile is crucial for staying competitive in local search results.

Managing multiple locations involves optimizing your site and GMB profile for each location. Creating separate pages for each location with unique content and NAP information can improve your local SEO. Ensuring each location's GMB profile is accurate and up-to-date is also important. Managing reviews and responding to them for each location can enhance your reputation and visibility. Optimizing for multiple locations requires careful planning and attention to detail but can significantly improve your local search presence.

Local link building involves earning backlinks from local websites and businesses. Building relationships with local bloggers, news sites, and industry associations can provide valuable backlink opportunities. Participating in local events, sponsorships, and community activities can also help you earn local backlinks. Local link building signals to Google that your site is relevant to users in your area. A strong local link-building strategy enhances your local SEO and improves your visibility in local search results.

Participating in local events can boost your local SEO by increasing your visibility and engagement with your community. Hosting or sponsoring local events, attending community activities, and partnering with local organizations can provide opportunities for earning backlinks and citations. Promoting your involvement in local events through your website and social media can attract local traffic and improve your local search rankings. Engaging with your community through local events enhances your local presence and builds relationships with local customers.

Community engagement is important for building a strong local presence. Engaging with your local audience through social media, local events, and community activities can improve your local SEO. Responding to comments, reviews, and messages promptly builds trust and credibility. Showing your involvement in the community through local content and promotions enhances your reputation and visibility. Community engagement is a valuable part of a successful local SEO strategy and helps you connect with your local audience.

Tracking local SEO performance helps you understand the effectiveness of your optimization efforts. Regularly monitoring your local search rankings, traffic, and engagement can provide insights into what's working and what needs improvement. Using tools like Google Analytics, Google Search Console, and local SEO tools can help you track your performance. Analyzing this data helps you make informed decisions and adjust your strategy as needed. Regular tracking and optimization ensure your local SEO remains effective and aligned with your goals.

Case studies of successful local SEO strategies provide valuable insights and inspiration. Analyzing how other businesses have achieved success with their local SEO efforts can help you refine your own strategy. Look for case studies that highlight different aspects of local SEO, such as GMB optimization, local content, or review management. Learning from real-world examples helps you understand best practices and avoid common pitfalls. Applying these lessons to your own strategy can improve your local SEO and overall performance.

Avoiding common local SEO mistakes is crucial for maintaining your rankings. Mistakes such as inconsistent NAP information, ignoring reviews, and poor mobile optimization can hurt your local search visibility. Regularly auditing your local SEO and fixing any issues can help maintain your rankings. Staying updated with best practices and algorithm changes is also important. By avoiding common mistakes and following best practices, you can enhance your local SEO and improve your site's visibility.

Optimizing for voice search is important for local SEO. Many local searches are performed using voice search, so ensuring your content is optimized for voice queries can improve your local search visibility. Voice search optimization involves using natural language, answering common questions, and providing clear and concise information. Including local keywords and creating FAQ pages can enhance your voice search optimization. Optimizing for voice search helps you reach more local customers and improve your local SEO.

The future of local SEO involves staying updated with industry trends and algorithm changes. As search engines continue to evolve, it's important to adapt your local SEO strategy to stay competitive. Focusing on providing value to your local audience, engaging with your community, and using ethical practices ensures your local SEO remains effective. Staying informed about changes in local search algorithms and best practices helps you maintain your local search visibility. The future of local SEO involves a more holistic and community-focused approach.

Tools for local SEO, such as Google My Business, Moz Local, and BrightLocal, can enhance your optimization efforts. These tools provide valuable insights, track performance, and help you manage your local SEO. Using tools effectively can streamline your local SEO process and improve your results. Leveraging technology and data can give you a competitive edge in local SEO. Investing in the right tools helps you optimize your local presence and attract more customers from your area.

In summary, local SEO involves optimizing your website and online presence to attract more business from relevant local searches. By focusing on key elements like Google My Business, local keywords, backlinks, and reviews, you can enhance your local SEO and provide a better user experience. Regularly tracking and optimizing your local SEO ensures it remains effective and aligned with your goals. A strong local SEO strategy is essential for attracting local customers and improving your visibility in local search results.

Chapter 8: Content Marketing and SEO

Content marketing is a powerful strategy for boosting your SEO and attracting more traffic to your website. It involves creating and sharing valuable, relevant, and consistent content to attract and engage your target audience. High-quality content not only provides value to your audience but also helps you rank higher in search results. Content marketing and SEO go hand in hand, as creating great content is essential for improving your search visibility and driving organic traffic.

Creating a content marketing strategy is the first step in using content to boost your SEO. This involves defining your goals, identifying your target audience, and planning your content. Your goals might include increasing website traffic, generating leads, or building brand awareness. Understanding your audience's needs, interests, and pain points helps you create content that resonates with them. Planning your content involves creating a content calendar and deciding on the types of content you'll produce. A well-defined strategy ensures your content marketing efforts are focused and effective.

Blog posts are a popular and effective form of content for boosting SEO. They provide an opportunity to target specific keywords, answer questions, and provide valuable information to your audience. Regularly publishing high-quality blog posts can improve your search rankings and attract more traffic to your site. Each blog post should be well-researched, informative, and optimized for your target keywords. Including images, videos, and internal links can enhance your blog posts and improve user engagement.

Videos are another powerful form of content for boosting SEO. Videos are highly engaging and can help you reach a broader audience on platforms like YouTube and social media. Creating informative and entertaining videos can attract more views and drive traffic to your site. Videos can also enhance your content by providing visual explanations of complex topics. Optimizing your videos for SEO involves using descriptive titles, tags, and descriptions that include your keywords. Embedding videos in your blog posts can improve user engagement and SEO.

Infographics are visually appealing and easy to share, making them a great tool for boosting SEO. They can simplify complex information and make it more digestible for your audience. Creating high-quality infographics that provide valuable information can attract backlinks and social shares, improving your SEO. Infographics can be used to summarize blog posts, present data, or explain processes. Optimizing your infographics for SEO involves using descriptive filenames, alt text, and embedding them in your content.

Podcasts are another effective form of content for reaching your audience and boosting SEO. Podcasts allow you to share your expertise, interview industry experts, and engage with your audience in a conversational format. Creating a podcast series on topics relevant to your audience can attract more listeners and drive traffic to your site. Optimizing your podcast for SEO involves using descriptive titles, tags, and show notes that include your keywords. Promoting your podcast on your website and social media can enhance its reach and impact.

Creating shareable content is important for boosting SEO. Shareable content is content that resonates with your audience and encourages them to share it with others. This can include blog posts, videos, infographics, and social media posts. Creating content that is informative, entertaining, or inspiring can increase its shareability. Encouraging social sharing by including share buttons and calls to action can amplify your content's reach. The more your content is shared, the more likely it is to attract backlinks and improve your SEO.

Content calendars are essential for planning and organizing your content marketing efforts. A content calendar helps you schedule and plan your content in advance, ensuring you consistently publish new and relevant content. It can include details such as content topics, formats, publication dates, and promotional strategies. Using a content calendar helps you stay organized and ensures your content marketing efforts are focused and aligned with your goals. Regularly reviewing and updating your content calendar ensures your content strategy remains effective.

Repurposing content involves reusing and repackaging your existing content in different formats. This can help you reach a wider audience and maximize the value of your content. For example, you can turn a blog post into a video, an infographic, or a podcast episode. Repurposing content allows you to present the same information in different ways, catering to different audience preferences. It also helps you save time and resources by making the most of your existing content. Repurposing content enhances your content marketing efforts and improves your SEO.

Content promotion is crucial for boosting your SEO. Creating great content is only half the battle; you also need to promote it to reach your target audience. Promoting your content involves sharing it on social media, sending it to your email list, and reaching out to influencers and bloggers. Using paid advertising, such as social media ads and Google Ads, can also increase your content's visibility. Effective content promotion amplifies your reach, attracts more traffic, and improves your SEO.

Guest blogging is a powerful strategy for content marketing and SEO. Writing articles for other blogs in your niche can help you reach a wider audience and earn high-quality backlinks. Guest blogging allows you to showcase your expertise and build relationships with other bloggers and influencers. To get started, identify reputable blogs in your niche and pitch them relevant and valuable content ideas. Writing high-quality guest posts can enhance your content marketing efforts and improve your SEO.

Content partnerships involve collaborating with other businesses, influencers, or organizations to create and promote content. Partnerships can help you reach a broader audience and enhance your content marketing efforts. Collaborating on content such as blog posts, videos, webinars, or eBooks can provide valuable insights and perspectives. Content partnerships also provide opportunities for earning backlinks and social shares. Building strong content partnerships can amplify your content's reach and improve your SEO.

Measuring content marketing success involves tracking key metrics to understand the effectiveness of your efforts. Important metrics include website traffic, engagement, social shares, and conversions. Using tools like Google Analytics, social media analytics, and SEO tools can provide valuable insights into your content's performance. Regularly reviewing your metrics helps you identify what's working and what needs improvement. Measuring your content marketing success ensures your efforts are focused and aligned with your goals.

Case studies of successful content marketing provide valuable insights and inspiration. Analyzing how other businesses have achieved success with their content marketing efforts can help you refine your own strategy. Look for case studies that highlight different aspects of content marketing, such as content creation, promotion, or partnerships. Learning from real-world examples helps you understand best practices and avoid common pitfalls. Applying these lessons to your own strategy can improve your content marketing efforts and overall SEO performance.

Writing SEO-friendly content involves using keywords naturally and strategically. Keywords should be placed in key areas such as the title, headings, meta descriptions, and throughout the body of the content. However, it's important to avoid keyword stuffing, which can lead to penalties. Instead, focus on creating high-quality content that addresses the user's needs and incorporates keywords seamlessly. The goal is to make your content relevant and valuable to both users and search engines.

Evergreen content is content that remains relevant and valuable over time. Unlike seasonal or trend-based content, evergreen content addresses timeless topics that continue to attract traffic long after it's published. Examples include how-to guides, tutorials, and FAQs. Creating evergreen content is a smart strategy for long-term SEO success. It provides ongoing value to your audience and continues to drive traffic to your site. By focusing on evergreen topics, you can build a strong foundation of high-quality content that stands the test of time.

Interactive content, such as quizzes, surveys, and calculators, can enhance your content marketing efforts and boost SEO. Interactive content engages your audience and encourages them to participate, increasing time on site and user interaction. Creating interactive content that provides value and entertainment can attract more traffic and social shares. Interactive content also provides valuable data and insights into your audience's preferences and behavior. Including interactive elements in your content strategy can enhance user experience and improve your SEO.

User-generated content involves content created by your audience, such as reviews, testimonials, and social media posts. Encouraging user-generated content can enhance your content marketing efforts and improve your SEO. User-generated content builds trust and credibility, as it provides authentic perspectives from real users. Promoting and sharing user-generated content can increase engagement and attract more traffic. Incorporating user-generated content into your strategy can enhance your content marketing efforts and boost your SEO.

Email marketing is an effective way to promote your content and engage with your audience. Sending newsletters, updates, and promotional emails can drive traffic to your site and improve your SEO. Building a strong email list and regularly sending valuable content to your subscribers can enhance your content marketing efforts. Email marketing allows you to reach your audience directly and keep them informed about your latest content and offers. Integrating email marketing into your content strategy can amplify your reach and improve your SEO.

Content updates involve regularly reviewing and refreshing your existing content to ensure it stays current and valuable. Over time, information can become outdated, and new trends can emerge. Regularly updating your content with new information, latest trends, and current data can improve your rankings. This doesn't mean you need to update your entire site frequently, but keeping key pages and popular posts current can make a big difference. Content updates signal to Google that your site is active and relevant.

Tools for content marketing, such as HubSpot, CoSchedule, and BuzzSumo, can enhance your efforts. These tools provide valuable insights, track performance, and help you manage your content marketing strategy. Using tools effectively can streamline your content marketing process and improve your results. Leveraging technology and data can give you a competitive edge in content marketing.

Investing in the right tools helps you create, promote, and measure your content more effectively.

To sum up, content marketing is a powerful strategy for boosting your SEO and attracting more traffic to your website. By focusing on creating high-quality, valuable content and promoting it effectively, you can enhance your search visibility and provide a better user experience. Regularly measuring and optimizing your content marketing efforts ensures they remain effective and aligned with your goals. A strong content marketing strategy is essential for long-term SEO success and online growth.

Chapter 9: Social Media and SEO

Social media and SEO are closely connected, and integrating social media into your SEO strategy can enhance your online presence and drive more traffic to your website. Social media platforms provide opportunities to share your content, engage with your audience, and build your brand. While social signals (likes, shares, and comments) are not direct ranking factors, they can indirectly impact your SEO by increasing your content's visibility and attracting backlinks. By leveraging social media effectively, you can boost your SEO efforts and improve your overall online performance.

Integrating social media into your SEO strategy involves creating and sharing content that resonates with your audience. This includes blog posts, videos, infographics, and social media posts. Sharing valuable and engaging content on social media can increase its reach and encourage more people to visit your website. Using relevant hashtags, engaging with your followers, and participating in conversations can enhance your social media presence and drive more traffic to your site. Consistent and strategic social media activity can amplify your SEO efforts and improve your search visibility.

Social sharing buttons make it easy for users to share your content on social media platforms. Including social sharing buttons on your blog posts, articles, and other content can increase its shareability and reach. When users share your content, it can attract more traffic and social signals, which can indirectly impact your SEO. Encouraging social sharing through calls to action and shareable content can enhance your content's visibility and attract more visitors to your site. Social sharing buttons are a simple but effective way to integrate social media into your SEO strategy.

Facebook is a powerful platform for boosting your SEO and reaching a broader audience. Sharing your content on Facebook can increase its visibility and attract more traffic to your site. Engaging with your followers through comments, likes, and shares can enhance your social media presence and build your brand. Facebook ads can also help you reach a targeted audience and drive more traffic to your website. Using Facebook effectively can amplify your SEO efforts and improve your overall online performance.

Twitter is another valuable platform for boosting your SEO. Sharing short, engaging updates and links to your content on Twitter can increase its reach and attract more visitors. Using relevant hashtags, participating in Twitter chats, and engaging with your followers can enhance your social media presence and drive more traffic to your site. Twitter's fast-paced nature allows you to share content frequently and reach a wide audience. Leveraging Twitter effectively can enhance your SEO strategy and improve your search visibility.

LinkedIn is a powerful platform for reaching a professional audience and boosting your SEO. Sharing valuable content, such as blog posts, industry news, and case studies, on LinkedIn can increase its reach and attract more traffic to your site. Engaging with your connections through comments, likes, and shares can enhance your social media presence and build your brand. LinkedIn groups provide opportunities to connect with like-minded professionals and share your content. Using LinkedIn effectively can amplify your SEO efforts and improve your overall online performance.

Instagram is a visually-driven platform that can enhance your SEO by increasing your content's visibility and engagement. Sharing high-quality images, videos, and stories on Instagram can attract more followers and drive traffic to your site. Using relevant hashtags, engaging with your audience through comments and likes, and collaborating with influencers can enhance your social media presence and build your brand. Instagram ads can also help you reach a targeted audience and drive more traffic to your website. Leveraging Instagram effectively can boost your SEO strategy and improve your search visibility.

Pinterest is another visually-driven platform that can boost your SEO. Sharing high-quality images, infographics, and visual content on Pinterest can increase its reach and attract more visitors to your site. Creating and optimizing pins with descriptive titles, keywords, and hashtags can enhance your content's visibility and improve your search rankings. Engaging with your audience through comments, repins, and likes can build your social media presence and drive more traffic to your site. Using Pinterest effectively can amplify your SEO efforts and improve your overall online performance.

Creating shareable content is important for integrating social media into your SEO strategy. Shareable content is content that resonates with your audience and encourages them to share it with others. This can include blog posts, videos, infographics, and social media posts. Creating content that is informative, entertaining, or inspiring can increase its shareability. Encouraging social sharing by including share buttons and calls to action can amplify your content's reach. The more your content is shared, the more likely it is to attract backlinks and improve your SEO.

Optimizing your social media profiles is crucial for enhancing your SEO. Your social media profiles should be complete, accurate, and consistent with your brand. This includes using a clear and descriptive username, profile picture, and bio. Including links to your website and other social media profiles can enhance your online presence and drive more traffic to your site. Optimizing your social media profiles helps search engines understand your brand and improves your search visibility.

Using hashtags effectively can enhance your social media presence and boost your SEO. Hashtags help categorize your content and make it discoverable to a broader audience. Using relevant and popular hashtags can increase the reach of your content and attract more followers. Creating branded hashtags can build your brand and encourage user-generated content. Monitoring and participating in trending hashtags can also increase your visibility and engagement. Using hashtags strategically can amplify your social media efforts and improve your SEO.

Social media analytics provide valuable insights into your social media performance and its impact on your SEO. Analyzing metrics such as engagement, reach, and traffic can help you understand what's working and what needs improvement. Tools like Google Analytics, social media analytics, and SEO tools can provide detailed reports on your social media activity. Regularly reviewing your analytics helps you make informed decisions and optimize your social media strategy. Using analytics effectively ensures your social media efforts are aligned with your SEO goals.

Social media can enhance your link-building efforts by increasing the visibility of your content and attracting backlinks. Sharing your content on social media platforms can attract the attention of bloggers, influencers, and other website owners. This can lead to more backlinks from reputable sources, which can improve your SEO. Engaging with your audience and building relationships with influencers can also provide backlink opportunities. Using social media to promote your content and connect with others can amplify your link-building efforts and improve your search visibility.

Social media engagement is important for building your brand and boosting your SEO. Engaging with your followers through comments, likes, and shares can enhance your social media presence and build relationships with your audience. Responding to comments and messages promptly builds trust and credibility. Creating interactive content, such as polls, quizzes, and contests, can increase engagement and attract more followers. Social media engagement provides valuable social signals that can indirectly impact your SEO.

Social media ads can help you reach a targeted audience and drive more traffic to your website. Platforms like Facebook, Instagram, Twitter, and LinkedIn offer various advertising options to promote your content and build your brand. Creating compelling ads that resonate with your audience can increase click-through rates and conversions. Using social media ads effectively can amplify your content's reach and enhance your SEO efforts. Investing in social media advertising can provide a significant boost to your online presence and search visibility.

Influencer marketing involves collaborating with influencers in your niche to promote your content and build your brand. Influencers have a large following and can amplify your content's reach and impact. Building relationships with influencers through social media, email, and networking can help you earn backlinks and attract more traffic to your site. Offering valuable content, collaborating on projects, or providing exclusive insights can incentivize influencers to share your content. Influencer marketing is a powerful strategy for boosting your SEO and increasing your content's visibility.

Tracking social media ROI (Return on Investment) helps you understand the effectiveness of your social media efforts. Measuring metrics such as engagement, traffic, conversions, and revenue can provide insights into your social media performance. Using tools like Google Analytics and social media analytics can help you track and measure your ROI. Regularly reviewing your metrics and adjusting your strategy ensures your social media efforts are focused and aligned with your goals. Tracking ROI helps you make informed decisions and optimize your social media strategy.

Case studies of successful social media SEO strategies provide valuable insights and inspiration. Analyzing how other businesses have achieved success with their social media efforts can help you refine your own strategy. Look for case studies that highlight different aspects of social media SEO, such as content creation, engagement, or influencer marketing. Learning from real-world examples helps you understand best practices and avoid common pitfalls. Applying these lessons to your own strategy can improve your social media efforts and overall SEO performance.

Common social media mistakes to avoid include inconsistent posting, ignoring engagement, and using irrelevant hashtags. Regularly posting valuable content, engaging with your audience, and using relevant hashtags can enhance your social media presence. Avoiding spammy or low-quality content, over-promotion, and ignoring analytics can also improve your social media strategy. By avoiding common mistakes and following best practices, you can enhance your social media efforts and boost your SEO.

The future of social media and SEO involves staying updated with industry trends and algorithm changes. As social media platforms and search engines continue to evolve, it's important to adapt your strategy to stay competitive. Focusing on providing value to your audience, engaging with your followers, and using ethical practices ensures your social media efforts remain effective. Staying informed about changes in social media algorithms and best practices helps you maintain your online presence. The future of social media and SEO involves a more integrated and user-focused approach.

Tools for social media marketing, such as Hootsuite, Buffer, and Sprout Social, can enhance your efforts. These tools provide valuable insights, track performance, and help you manage your social media strategy. Using tools effectively can streamline your social media process and improve your results. Leveraging technology and data can give you a competitive edge in social media marketing. Investing in the right tools helps you create, promote, and measure your social media efforts more effectively.

In summary, social media and SEO are closely connected, and integrating social media into your SEO strategy can enhance your online presence and drive more traffic to your website. By creating and sharing valuable content, engaging with your audience, and using effective strategies, you can boost your SEO efforts and improve your search visibility. Regularly measuring and optimizing your social media efforts ensures they remain effective and aligned with your goals. A strong social media strategy is essential for long-term SEO success and online growth.

Chapter 10: Measuring and Analyzing SEO Performance

Measuring and analyzing SEO performance is crucial for understanding the effectiveness of your efforts and making informed decisions. SEO is an ongoing process, and regularly tracking your performance helps you identify what's working and what needs improvement. Using tools like Google Analytics, Google Search Console, and other SEO tools provides valuable insights into your site's performance, traffic, and rankings. By analyzing this data, you can optimize your strategy and achieve better results.

Tracking key SEO metrics helps you understand the effectiveness of your optimization efforts. Important metrics include organic traffic, keyword rankings, bounce rate, time on site, and conversions. Organic traffic refers to the number of visitors who find your site through search engines. Keyword rankings show how your site ranks for specific search queries. Bounce rate indicates the percentage of visitors who leave your site after viewing only one page. Time on site measures how long visitors stay on your site. Conversions track the number of visitors who complete a desired action, such as making a purchase or filling out a form. Monitoring these metrics helps you understand your site's performance and make informed decisions.

Google Analytics is a powerful tool for tracking and analyzing your site's performance. It provides detailed reports on traffic, user behavior, and conversions. Using Google Analytics, you can track key metrics, set up goals, and create custom reports. The data from Google Analytics helps you understand how visitors interact with your site and identify areas for improvement. Regularly reviewing your Google Analytics data ensures your SEO strategy is focused and effective.

Google Search Console is another valuable tool for monitoring your site's SEO performance. It provides insights into your site's search traffic, indexing status, and technical issues. Using Google Search Console, you can track keyword rankings, submit sitemaps, and monitor backlinks. The data from Google Search Console helps you identify and fix issues that may impact your site's performance. Regularly reviewing your Google Search Console data ensures your site is optimized and aligned with best practices.

Tracking keyword rankings helps you understand how your site is performing for specific search queries. Using tools like Ahrefs, SEMrush, and Moz, you can monitor your keyword rankings and track changes over time. This data helps you identify which keywords are driving traffic and which need improvement. Regularly reviewing your keyword rankings ensures your content is optimized and relevant to your target audience. Tracking keyword performance is essential for maintaining and improving your search visibility.

Backlink analysis helps you understand the quality and impact of your backlinks. Using tools like Ahrefs, Moz, and Majestic, you can monitor your backlink profile and identify opportunities for improvement. This data helps you understand which backlinks are driving traffic and which may be harmful. Regularly reviewing your backlink profile ensures your links are from reputable sources and aligned with best practices. Backlink analysis is crucial for maintaining a healthy backlink profile and improving your SEO.

Content performance analysis helps you understand how your content is resonating with your audience. Using tools like Google Analytics and SEO tools, you can track metrics such as page views, time on page, and social shares. This data helps you identify which content is performing well and which needs improvement. Regularly reviewing your content performance ensures your content strategy is effective and aligned with your audience's needs. Content performance analysis is essential for creating high-quality, engaging content that drives traffic and conversions.

User behavior metrics provide insights into how visitors interact with your site. Important metrics include bounce rate, time on site, pages per session, and exit rate. Bounce rate indicates the percentage of visitors who leave your site after viewing only one page. Time on site measures how long visitors stay on your site. Pages per session tracks the average number of pages viewed per visit. Exit rate shows the percentage of visitors who leave your site from a specific page. Analyzing user behavior metrics helps you understand your audience's preferences and optimize your site for better engagement.

Tracking mobile SEO performance is crucial for understanding how your site performs on mobile devices. With more people using smartphones to browse the web, ensuring your site is mobile-friendly is essential. Using tools like Google Analytics and Google Search Console, you can monitor your mobile traffic, user behavior, and keyword rankings. This data helps you identify areas for improvement and optimize your site for mobile users. Regularly reviewing your mobile SEO performance ensures your site provides a seamless experience for all users.

Local SEO metrics help you understand how your site is performing for local search queries. Important metrics include local keyword rankings, Google My Business insights, and local traffic. Using tools like Google Analytics, Google Search Console, and local SEO tools, you can monitor your local SEO performance and identify opportunities for improvement. Regularly reviewing your local SEO metrics ensures your site is optimized for local search and attracts more local customers. Local SEO performance analysis is essential for businesses that serve specific geographic areas.

Heatmaps provide visual insights into how visitors interact with your site. Using tools like Hotjar and Crazy Egg, you can track user clicks, scrolls, and movements. Heatmaps help you understand which elements of your site are attracting attention and which are being ignored. This data helps you identify areas for improvement and optimize your site for better engagement. Regularly reviewing your heatmaps ensures your site is user-friendly and aligned with your audience's preferences. Heatmaps are a valuable tool for understanding user behavior and improving your site's performance.

Conversion rate optimization (CRO) involves improving your site's ability to convert visitors into customers or leads. Using tools like Google Analytics, Optimizely, and Unbounce, you can track conversions and identify areas for improvement. CRO involves analyzing user behavior, testing different elements, and optimizing your site for better performance. Regularly reviewing your conversion data ensures your site is effective at achieving your goals. Conversion rate optimization is essential for maximizing the value of your traffic and improving your site's performance.

Setting up SEO goals helps you measure the success of your optimization efforts. Your goals might include increasing organic traffic, improving keyword rankings, reducing bounce rate, or boosting conversions. Using tools like Google Analytics and SEO tools, you can track your progress towards these goals and make informed decisions. Setting up specific, measurable, achievable, relevant, and time-bound (SMART) goals ensures your SEO strategy is focused and effective. Regularly reviewing and adjusting your goals ensures your efforts are aligned with your overall business objectives.

SEO dashboards provide a centralized view of your key metrics and performance data. Using tools like Google Data Studio, Tableau, and Cyfe, you can create custom dashboards that track your SEO performance. Dashboards help you visualize your data and identify trends and opportunities for improvement. Regularly reviewing your SEO dashboards ensures your strategy is effective and aligned with your goals. SEO dashboards are a valuable tool for monitoring your performance and making informed decisions.

Creating SEO reports helps you communicate your performance and progress to stakeholders. Using tools like Google Analytics, Google Search Console, and SEO tools, you can generate detailed reports on your key metrics and performance data. SEO reports provide insights into your traffic, rankings, user behavior, and conversions. Regularly creating and sharing SEO reports ensures transparency and accountability. SEO reports help you track your progress, identify areas for improvement, and make data-driven decisions.

A/B testing involves comparing two versions of a page or element to see which performs better. Using tools like Optimizely, VWO, and Google Optimize, you can run A/B tests on different elements of your site, such as headlines, images, and calls to action. A/B testing helps you understand which changes improve user engagement and conversions. Regularly conducting A/B tests ensures your site is optimized for better performance. A/B testing is a valuable tool for improving your SEO and user experience.

Competitor analysis helps you understand how your site compares to others in your niche. Using tools like Ahrefs, SEMrush, and Moz, you can analyze your competitors' backlinks, keyword rankings, and content. This data helps you identify opportunities for improvement and refine your strategy. Regularly reviewing your competitor analysis ensures your site stays competitive and aligned with industry trends. Competitor analysis is essential for understanding your strengths and weaknesses and improving your SEO performance.

Tracking social media impact on SEO helps you understand how your social media efforts influence your search performance. Using tools like Google Analytics and social media analytics, you can monitor the traffic, engagement, and conversions generated from your social media channels. This data helps you identify which social media activities are driving the most value and optimize your strategy. Regularly reviewing your social media impact ensures your efforts are effective and aligned with your SEO goals. Social media impact analysis is essential for integrating social media into your SEO strategy.

Regular SEO audits help you maintain and improve your site's performance. An SEO audit involves reviewing all aspects of your optimization, including technical elements, content, backlinks, and user experience. Using tools like Google Analytics, Google Search Console, and SEO tools, you can identify issues and opportunities for improvement. Regularly conducting SEO audits ensures your site stays up-to-date with best practices and algorithm changes. SEO audits are essential for maintaining your rankings and providing a better user experience.

Adjusting your SEO strategy based on data helps you achieve better results. Regularly reviewing your performance data and making informed decisions ensures your efforts are focused and effective. This involves analyzing key metrics, identifying trends, and implementing changes. Adjusting your strategy based on data helps you stay competitive and achieve your goals. Continuous optimization and adaptation are key to long-term SEO success.

SEO analysis tools provide valuable insights into your site's performance and opportunities for improvement. Using tools like Google Analytics, Google Search Console, Ahrefs, SEMrush, and Moz, you can track your metrics, monitor your rankings, and analyze your backlinks. These tools help you make data-driven decisions and optimize your strategy. Regularly using SEO analysis tools ensures your site stays competitive and aligned with best practices. Investing in the right tools helps you measure and analyze your SEO performance more effectively.

To sum up, measuring and analyzing SEO performance is crucial for understanding the effectiveness of your efforts and making informed decisions. By tracking key metrics, using the right tools, and regularly reviewing your data, you can optimize your strategy and achieve better results. Continuous measurement and analysis ensure your SEO efforts are focused and aligned with your goals. A data-driven approach to SEO is essential for long-term success and online growth.

Chapter 11: Voice Search Optimization

Voice search optimization is an essential aspect of modern SEO, as more people use voice assistants like Siri, Alexa, and Google Assistant to search the web. Voice search queries are typically longer and more conversational than text searches, requiring a different approach to optimization. By optimizing your site for voice search, you can improve your visibility and reach a broader audience. Understanding how voice search works and implementing effective strategies can enhance your SEO and provide a better user experience.

Voice search works by using natural language processing and artificial intelligence to understand and respond to user queries. When users speak into their devices, the voice assistant processes the query, searches the web, and delivers the most relevant results. Voice search queries often include question words like "who," "what," "where," "when," "why," and "how." Optimizing your content to answer these questions can improve your chances of appearing in voice search results.

Optimizing for voice search involves using natural language and conversational keywords. Voice search queries are typically longer and more conversational than text searches, so using natural language in your content is crucial. This means writing in a conversational tone and using phrases that people are likely to speak. For example, instead of using the keyword "best pizza NYC," you might use "where can I find the best pizza in New York City?" Including long-tail keywords and conversational phrases in your content can improve your voice search optimization.

Featured snippets play a significant role in voice search optimization. Featured snippets are concise answers that appear at the top of search results, often referred to as "position zero." Voice assistants frequently use featured snippets to provide answers to voice queries. Optimizing your content to appear in featured snippets can increase your chances of being featured in voice search results. This involves creating clear and concise answers to common questions, using bullet points or numbered lists, and structuring your content effectively.

Using schema markup can enhance your voice search optimization. Schema markup is a type of structured data that helps search engines understand the content on your site better. Using schema markup, you can provide additional information about your content, such as product details, reviews, and events. This helps search engines display rich snippets in search results, which can improve your click-through rates and visibility. Implementing schema markup involves adding specific code to your pages that tells search engines what the content is about. Local schema markup enhances your local SEO and provides more detailed information to users.

Mobile optimization is crucial for voice search, as most voice searches are performed on mobile devices. Ensuring your site is mobile-friendly, with a responsive design, fast loading times, and easy navigation, is essential for voice search optimization. Google uses mobile-first indexing, which means it primarily uses the mobile version of your site for ranking and indexing. Optimizing your site for mobile users ensures a seamless experience and improves your chances of ranking in voice search results.

Creating voice-friendly content involves answering common questions clearly and concisely. Voice search queries often include question words like "who," "what," "where," "when," "why," and "how." Structuring your content to address these questions can improve your voice search optimization. Using headings, subheadings, bullet points, and numbered lists can make your content more scannable and easier for search engines to understand. Voice-friendly content provides valuable information in a clear and concise manner, enhancing your SEO and user experience.

Local SEO plays a significant role in voice search optimization, as many voice searches have local intent. People often use voice search to find nearby businesses, services, and places. Optimizing your site for local keywords, claiming and optimizing your Google My Business profile, and getting listed in local directories can improve your local voice search rankings. Ensuring your NAP (name, address, phone number) information is accurate and consistent across the web is crucial for local SEO and voice search optimization.

Tracking voice search performance helps you understand how your site is performing for voice queries. Using tools like Google Analytics and Google Search Console, you can monitor your voice search traffic, user behavior, and keyword rankings. This data helps you identify areas for improvement and optimize your site for voice search. Regularly reviewing your voice search performance ensures your site is optimized and aligned with best practices. Voice search performance analysis is essential for staying competitive and improving your search visibility.

Case studies of successful voice search optimization provide valuable insights and inspiration. Analyzing how other businesses have achieved success with their voice search efforts can help you refine your own strategy. Look for case studies that highlight different aspects of voice search optimization, such as content creation, local SEO, or schema markup. Learning from real-world examples helps you understand best practices and avoid common pitfalls. Applying these lessons to your own strategy can improve your voice search optimization and overall SEO performance.

Common voice search mistakes to avoid include using overly technical language, neglecting mobile optimization, and ignoring local SEO.

Ensuring your content is written in natural language, optimized for mobile devices, and targeted for local search is crucial for voice search optimization. Regularly auditing your site and fixing any issues can help maintain your rankings. Staying updated with best practices and algorithm changes is also important. By avoiding common mistakes and following best practices, you can enhance your voice search optimization and improve your site's visibility.

The future of voice search involves staying updated with industry trends and advancements in artificial intelligence and natural language processing. As voice search continues to grow, it's important to adapt your SEO strategy to stay competitive. Focusing on providing value to your audience, using natural language, and optimizing for mobile users ensures your voice search efforts remain effective. Staying informed about changes in voice search algorithms and best practices helps you maintain your online presence. The future of voice search involves a more conversational and user-focused approach.

Tools for voice search optimization, such as Google Analytics, Google Search Console, and schema markup generators, can enhance your efforts. These tools provide valuable insights, track performance, and help you implement effective voice search strategies. Using tools effectively can streamline your voice search optimization process and improve your results. Leveraging technology and data can give you a competitive edge in voice search optimization. Investing in the right tools helps you measure and analyze your voice search performance more effectively.

Integrating voice search into your overall SEO strategy involves aligning your efforts with your broader SEO goals. This includes optimizing your content, site structure, and technical elements for both text and voice searches. Ensuring your SEO strategy is comprehensive and includes voice search optimization helps you reach a wider audience and improve your search visibility. Regularly reviewing and adjusting your strategy based on performance data ensures your efforts are effective and aligned with your goals. A holistic approach to SEO that includes voice search optimization is essential for long-term success.

Voice search and e-commerce are closely connected, as more people use voice assistants to search for products and make purchases. Optimizing your e-commerce site for voice search involves using natural language, answering common questions, and providing detailed product information. Ensuring your site is mobile-friendly and optimized for local search can also improve your voice search rankings. Voice search optimization for e-commerce helps you reach more customers and improve your sales.

Using FAQs for voice search involves creating detailed and informative FAQ pages that answer common questions. FAQs are a valuable resource for voice search optimization, as they provide clear and concise answers that match voice search queries. Including long-tail keywords and conversational phrases in your FAQs can improve your chances of appearing in voice search results. Regularly updating your FAQs with new questions and answers ensures they remain relevant and valuable.

Fast-loading pages are crucial for voice search optimization, as users expect quick and accurate results. Ensuring your site loads quickly on both desktop and mobile devices can improve your voice search rankings. Optimizing images, leveraging browser caching, and reducing server response times can enhance your site's speed. Fast-loading pages provide a better user experience and increase your chances of ranking in voice search results.

Voice search optimization involves continuously monitoring and adjusting your strategy based on performance data. Regularly reviewing your voice search metrics and making informed decisions ensures your efforts are focused and effective. This involves analyzing key metrics, identifying trends, and implementing changes. Continuous optimization and adaptation are key to long-term voice search success. A data-driven approach to voice search optimization is essential for improving your search visibility and online performance.

To sum up, voice search optimization is an essential aspect of modern SEO. By understanding how voice search works and implementing effective strategies, you can improve your visibility and reach a broader audience. Focusing on natural language, mobile optimization, and local SEO ensures your voice search efforts are effective and aligned with best practices. Regularly measuring and optimizing your voice search performance helps you stay competitive and achieve better results. Voice search optimization is crucial for long-term SEO success and online growth.

Chapter 12: Mobile SEO Best Practices

Mobile SEO is essential in today's digital landscape, as more people use smartphones and tablets to browse the web. Ensuring your site is optimized for mobile devices can improve your search visibility and provide a better user experience. Google uses mobile-first indexing, which means it primarily uses the mobile version of your site for ranking and indexing. By implementing effective mobile SEO strategies, you can enhance your site's performance and reach a broader audience.

Mobile-first indexing involves Google primarily using the mobile version of your site for ranking and indexing. This means your site needs to be fully optimized for mobile devices to perform well in search results. Ensuring your site is mobile-friendly, with a responsive design, fast loading times, and easy navigation, is crucial for mobile SEO. Regularly reviewing and updating your mobile site ensures it meets Google's standards and provides a seamless experience for users.

Responsive design is a key factor in mobile SEO. A responsive site automatically adjusts its layout and content to fit different screen sizes, providing a consistent experience across devices. Using responsive design ensures your site is accessible and user-friendly on both desktop and mobile devices. This involves using flexible grids, images, and media queries to create a seamless experience. Implementing responsive design enhances your site's usability and improves your mobile SEO.

Optimizing for mobile speed is essential for providing a good user experience and improving your rankings. Fast-loading pages are crucial for mobile users, who expect quick and seamless browsing. Optimizing images, leveraging browser caching, and reducing server response times can enhance your site's speed. Using tools like Google PageSpeed Insights can help you identify areas for improvement and optimize your site for faster loading times. Ensuring your site loads quickly on mobile devices improves your mobile SEO and user experience.

Mobile-friendly content involves creating content that is easily readable and accessible on small screens. This includes using larger fonts, shorter paragraphs, and clear headings to improve readability. Avoiding large blocks of text and using bullet points or numbered lists can make your content more scannable. Including images and videos that are optimized for mobile devices can enhance your content. Creating mobile-friendly content ensures a better user experience and improves your mobile SEO.

Accelerated Mobile Pages (AMP) is a framework that helps create fast-loading mobile pages. Implementing AMP can improve your site's mobile performance and rankings. AMP pages are lightweight and designed to load quickly on mobile devices. Using AMP involves creating a separate version of your content with specific HTML, CSS, and JavaScript. Implementing AMP can enhance your mobile SEO and provide a better experience for users. Faster mobile pages can improve your rankings and keep users engaged.

Mobile user experience (UX) is a major factor in mobile SEO. Good UX means users can easily navigate your site, find the information they need, and have a pleasant experience overall. Factors like site design, content layout, and ease of use all contribute to UX. Google measures UX using metrics such as bounce rate, time on site, and pages per session. A well-designed mobile site with high-quality content and easy navigation will keep users engaged and improve your rankings.

Mobile navigation involves creating a user-friendly and intuitive navigation system for mobile devices. This includes using clear and concise menu items, avoiding dropdown menus, and providing easy access to important pages. Ensuring your navigation is simple and easy to use can improve your site's usability and mobile SEO. Using a sticky navigation bar that remains visible as users scroll can enhance the user experience. Mobile navigation is crucial for helping users find what they need quickly and efficiently.

Optimizing mobile images involves using high-quality images that load quickly on mobile devices. This includes compressing images to reduce file size, using appropriate formats, and optimizing alt text for SEO. Ensuring your images are responsive and adjust to different screen sizes can improve your site's performance. Including descriptive filenames and alt text that include your keywords can enhance your mobile SEO. Properly optimized images provide a better user experience and improve your search visibility.

Using mobile-specific keywords can enhance your mobile SEO. Mobile users often use different keywords and search phrases than desktop users, such as shorter queries or voice search. Conducting keyword research to identify mobile-specific keywords can help you optimize your content for mobile users. Including these keywords naturally in your content, meta tags, and headings can improve your mobile rankings. Targeting mobile-specific keywords ensures your content is relevant and valuable to mobile users.

Local SEO plays a significant role in mobile SEO, as many mobile searches have local intent. People often use their smartphones to find nearby businesses, services, and places. Optimizing your site for local keywords, claiming and optimizing your Google My Business profile, and getting listed in local directories can improve your local mobile SEO. Ensuring your NAP (name, address, phone number) information is accurate and consistent across the web is crucial for local SEO and mobile optimization.

Tracking mobile SEO performance helps you understand how your site performs on mobile devices. Using tools like Google Analytics and Google Search Console, you can monitor your mobile traffic, user behavior, and keyword rankings. This data helps you identify areas for improvement and optimize your site for mobile users. Regularly reviewing your mobile SEO performance ensures your site provides a seamless experience for all users. Mobile SEO performance analysis is essential for staying competitive and improving your search visibility.

Case studies of successful mobile SEO provide valuable insights and inspiration. Analyzing how other businesses have achieved success with their mobile SEO efforts can help you refine your own strategy. Look for case studies that highlight different aspects of mobile SEO, such as responsive design, mobile speed optimization, or local SEO. Learning from real-world examples helps you understand best practices and avoid common pitfalls. Applying these lessons to your own strategy can improve your mobile SEO and overall performance.

Common mobile SEO mistakes to avoid include slow loading times, poor navigation, and unoptimized content. Ensuring your site loads quickly, has a user-friendly navigation system, and provides readable and accessible content is crucial for mobile SEO. Regularly auditing your site and fixing any issues can help maintain your rankings. Staying updated with best practices and algorithm changes is also important. By avoiding common mistakes and following best practices, you can enhance your mobile SEO and improve your site's visibility.

The future of mobile SEO involves staying updated with industry trends and advancements in mobile technology. As mobile usage continues to grow, it's important to adapt your SEO strategy to stay competitive. Focusing on providing value to your audience, using responsive design, and optimizing for mobile speed ensures your mobile SEO efforts remain effective. Staying informed about changes in mobile algorithms and best practices helps you maintain your online presence. The future of mobile SEO involves a more user-focused and mobile-first approach.

Tools for mobile SEO, such as Google Analytics, Google Search Console, and mobile speed optimization tools, can enhance your efforts. These tools provide valuable insights, track performance, and help you implement effective mobile SEO strategies. Using tools effectively can streamline your mobile SEO process and improve your results. Leveraging technology and data can give you a competitive edge in mobile SEO. Investing in the right tools helps you measure and analyze your mobile SEO performance more effectively.

Integrating mobile SEO into your overall SEO strategy involves aligning your efforts with your broader SEO goals. This includes optimizing your content, site structure, and technical elements for both desktop and mobile searches. Ensuring your SEO strategy is comprehensive and includes mobile SEO helps you reach a wider audience and improve your search visibility. Regularly reviewing and adjusting your strategy based on performance data ensures your efforts are effective and aligned with your goals. A holistic approach to SEO that includes mobile SEO is essential for long-term success.

To sum up, mobile SEO is essential in today's digital landscape. By implementing effective strategies and staying updated with best practices, you can improve your site's performance and reach a broader audience. Focusing on responsive design, mobile speed, and user experience ensures your mobile SEO efforts are effective and aligned with best practices. Regularly measuring and optimizing your mobile SEO performance helps you stay competitive and achieve better results. Mobile SEO is crucial for long-term SEO success and online growth.

Chapter 13: E-commerce SEO Strategies

E-commerce SEO is essential for online stores to attract more customers and increase sales. Optimizing your e-commerce site involves various strategies, such as keyword research, product page optimization, technical SEO, and content marketing. By implementing effective e-commerce SEO strategies, you can improve your search visibility, drive more traffic to your site, and boost your sales. Understanding how to optimize your e-commerce site can enhance your online presence and provide a better shopping experience for your customers.

Keyword research is the foundation of e-commerce SEO. Identifying relevant and high-converting keywords helps you optimize your product pages and attract more traffic. This involves researching product-specific keywords, long-tail keywords, and transactional keywords that indicate purchase intent. Using tools like Google Keyword Planner, Ahrefs, and SEMrush can help you find valuable keywords for your products. Regularly updating your keyword research ensures your content remains relevant and competitive.

Optimizing product pages involves using keywords naturally and strategically in key areas such as titles, descriptions, headings, and meta tags. Each product page should have a unique and descriptive title that includes your main keyword. Writing detailed and informative product descriptions that highlight the features and benefits of your products can enhance your SEO. Including high-quality images, videos, and customer reviews can improve user engagement and boost your rankings. Product page optimization is crucial for improving your search visibility and attracting more customers.

Technical SEO for e-commerce involves optimizing your site's infrastructure to improve its visibility and performance. This includes optimizing site speed, ensuring mobile-friendliness, and improving site architecture. Using tools like Google PageSpeed Insights, Google Search Console, and SEO tools can help you identify technical issues and optimize your site. Regularly reviewing and updating your technical SEO ensures your site meets best practices and provides a seamless shopping experience for your customers.

Content marketing is a powerful strategy for e-commerce SEO. Creating valuable and informative content, such as blog posts, guides, and videos, can attract more traffic and build your brand. This content can target long-tail keywords, answer common questions, and provide valuable information to your audience. Promoting your content through social media, email marketing, and influencer outreach can increase its visibility and drive more traffic to your site. Content marketing enhances your e-commerce SEO and provides valuable information to your customers.

Optimizing product images involves using high-quality images that load quickly and are optimized for SEO. This includes using descriptive filenames and alt text that include your keywords. Compressing images to reduce file size can improve page load times, which is crucial for user experience and SEO. Including multiple images from different angles and using zoom features can enhance the shopping experience. Properly optimized images provide a better user experience and improve your search visibility.

Using schema markup can enhance your e-commerce SEO by providing additional information about your products to search engines. This includes product details, reviews, prices, and availability. Implementing schema markup involves adding specific code to your product pages that tells search engines what the content is about. This helps search engines display rich snippets in search results, which can improve your click-through rates and visibility. Schema markup enhances your search presence and provides more detailed information to users.

Internal linking involves linking to other pages on your site to help users navigate and find related products. Using internal links strategically can improve your site's SEO and keep shoppers on your site longer. Linking to related products, categories, and blog posts provides additional value to your customers and enhances their shopping experience. Internal linking helps search engines understand your site's structure and discover new pages. It's a simple but powerful way to boost your SEO and engagement.

Customer reviews play a significant role in e-commerce SEO. Positive reviews from satisfied customers can enhance your reputation and improve your search rankings. Encouraging customers to leave reviews and responding to them promptly can build trust and credibility. Google considers reviews as a ranking factor, so having a high volume of positive reviews can boost your e-commerce SEO. Managing your online reviews effectively is essential for attracting more customers and improving your search visibility.

Optimizing your site for mobile users is crucial for e-commerce SEO. Many shoppers use their smartphones to browse and purchase products, so ensuring your site is mobile-friendly is essential. This includes using responsive design, fast loading times, and easy navigation. Ensuring your content is readable on small screens and providing a seamless mobile shopping experience can improve your mobile rankings. Google uses mobile-first indexing, which means it primarily uses the mobile version of your site for ranking and indexing. Optimizing your site for mobile users is crucial for staying competitive in search results.

Using social media to promote your products can enhance your e-commerce SEO. Sharing your products on social media platforms can increase their visibility and attract more traffic to your site. Engaging with your audience through comments, likes, and shares can build your social media presence and drive more traffic. Collaborating with influencers and running social media ads can amplify your reach and attract more customers. Using social media effectively can boost your e-commerce SEO and improve your search visibility.

Creating shareable content is important for e-commerce SEO. Shareable content is content that resonates with your audience and encourages them to share it with others. This can include blog posts, videos, infographics, and social media posts. Creating content that is informative, entertaining, or inspiring can increase its shareability. Encouraging social sharing by including share buttons and calls to action can amplify your content's reach. The more your content is shared, the more likely it is to attract backlinks and improve your SEO.

Using structured data helps search engines understand the content on your site better. Structured data, such as schema markup, provides additional information about your products, such as prices, reviews, and availability. This helps search engines display rich snippets in search results, which can improve your click-through rates and visibility. Implementing structured data involves adding specific code to your product pages that tells search engines what the content is about. Properly using structured data enhances your search presence and provides more detailed information to users.

Email marketing is an effective way to promote your products and engage with your customers. Sending newsletters, updates, and promotional emails can drive traffic to your site and improve your SEO. Building a strong email list and regularly sending valuable content to your subscribers can enhance your e-commerce SEO. Email marketing allows you to reach your audience directly and keep them informed about your latest products and offers. Integrating email marketing into your SEO strategy can amplify your reach and improve your search visibility.

Local SEO is important for e-commerce businesses that serve specific geographic areas. Optimizing your site for local keywords, claiming and optimizing your Google My Business profile, and getting listed in local directories can improve your local SEO. Ensuring your NAP (name, address, phone number) information is accurate and consistent across the web is crucial for local SEO. Local SEO helps you reach potential customers in your area and improves your visibility in local search results.

Tracking e-commerce SEO performance helps you understand the effectiveness of your optimization efforts. Using tools like Google Analytics, Google Search Console, and e-commerce SEO tools, you can monitor your traffic, keyword rankings, and conversions. This data helps you identify areas for improvement and optimize your site for better performance. Regularly reviewing your e-commerce SEO performance ensures your efforts are focused and aligned with your goals. E-commerce SEO performance analysis is essential for staying competitive and improving your search visibility.

Case studies of successful e-commerce SEO strategies provide valuable insights and inspiration. Analyzing how other online stores have achieved success with their SEO efforts can help you refine your own strategy. Look for case studies that highlight different aspects of e-commerce SEO, such as product page optimization, content marketing, or social media promotion. Learning from real-world examples helps you understand best practices and avoid common pitfalls. Applying these lessons to your own strategy can improve your e-commerce SEO and overall performance.

Common e-commerce SEO mistakes to avoid include duplicate content, slow loading times, and unoptimized product pages. Ensuring your site is free of duplicate content, loads quickly, and provides detailed and optimized product information is crucial for e-commerce SEO. Regularly auditing your site and fixing any issues can help maintain your rankings. Staying updated with best practices and algorithm changes is also important. By avoiding common mistakes and following best practices, you can enhance your e-commerce SEO and improve your site's visibility.

The future of e-commerce SEO involves staying updated with industry trends and advancements in technology. As e-commerce continues to grow, it's important to adapt your SEO strategy to stay competitive. Focusing on providing value to your customers, using responsive design, and optimizing for mobile users ensures your e-commerce SEO efforts remain effective. Staying informed about changes in search algorithms and best practices helps you maintain your online presence. The future of e-commerce SEO involves a more user-focused and data-driven approach.

Tools for e-commerce SEO, such as Google Analytics, Google Search Console, and e-commerce SEO tools, can enhance your efforts. These tools provide valuable insights, track performance, and help you implement effective e-commerce SEO strategies. Using tools effectively can streamline your e-commerce SEO process and improve your results. Leveraging technology and data can give you a competitive edge in e-commerce SEO. Investing in the right tools helps you measure and analyze your e-commerce SEO performance more effectively.

Integrating e-commerce SEO into your overall SEO strategy involves aligning your efforts with your broader SEO goals. This includes optimizing your content, site structure, and technical elements for both desktop and mobile searches. Ensuring your SEO strategy is comprehensive and includes e-commerce SEO helps you reach a wider audience and improve your search visibility. Regularly reviewing and adjusting your strategy based on performance data ensures your efforts are effective and aligned with your goals. A holistic approach to SEO that includes e-commerce SEO is essential for long-term success.

To sum up, e-commerce SEO is essential for online stores to attract more customers and increase sales. By implementing effective strategies and staying updated with best practices, you can improve your search visibility, drive more traffic to your site, and boost your sales. Focusing on keyword research, product page optimization, technical SEO, and content marketing ensures your e-commerce SEO efforts are effective and aligned with best practices. Regularly measuring and optimizing your e-commerce SEO performance helps you stay competitive and achieve better results. E-commerce SEO is crucial for long-term success and online growth.

Chapter 14: SEO for Blog Growth

SEO for blog growth involves optimizing your blog to attract more traffic, engage your audience, and build your brand. Blogging is a powerful tool for SEO, as it allows you to create valuable content that targets specific keywords, answers questions, and provides information to your audience. By implementing effective blog SEO strategies, you can improve your search visibility, drive more traffic to your site, and grow your blog. Understanding how to optimize your blog can enhance your online presence and provide a better experience for your readers.

Keyword research is the foundation of blog SEO. Identifying relevant and high-traffic keywords helps you create content that attracts more visitors and ranks higher in search results. This involves researching long-tail keywords, question-based keywords, and informational keywords that match user intent. Using tools like Google Keyword Planner, Ahrefs, and SEMrush can help you find valuable keywords for your blog posts. Regularly updating your keyword research ensures your content remains relevant and competitive.

Creating high-quality content is essential for blog SEO. Your blog posts should be well-researched, informative, and engaging. Writing detailed and valuable content that answers questions, provides insights, and solves problems can attract more readers and keep them coming back. Using a conversational tone and including personal anecdotes can make your content more relatable and enjoyable. High-quality content enhances your blog's SEO and builds trust with your audience.

Optimizing your blog posts involves using keywords naturally and strategically in key areas such as titles, headings, meta descriptions, and throughout the content. Each blog post should have a unique and descriptive title that includes your main keyword. Writing clear and concise meta descriptions that summarize your content and include your keywords can improve your click-through rates. Using headings and subheadings to structure your content makes it easier to read and understand. Properly optimized blog posts improve your search visibility and attract more traffic.

Creating compelling headlines is crucial for attracting readers to your blog posts. A good headline grabs attention, sparks curiosity, and encourages people to click. It should be clear, concise, and include your main keyword. Using numbers, questions, and power words can make your headlines more appealing. Spending time crafting your headlines can significantly improve your content's click-through rate and overall performance.

Using images and videos in your blog posts can enhance your content and improve user engagement. Visuals help illustrate your points, break up text, and make your content more appealing. Including high-quality images, infographics, and videos that are relevant to your content can keep readers engaged and provide additional value. Optimizing your images and videos for SEO by using descriptive filenames, alt text, and captions can improve your search visibility.

Internal linking involves linking to other relevant blog posts and pages on your site. This helps users navigate your blog, find related content, and stay on your site longer. Using internal links strategically can improve your blog's SEO and keep readers engaged. Linking to your most valuable and relevant content provides additional value to your readers and enhances their experience. Internal linking helps search engines understand your site's structure and discover new pages. It's a simple but powerful way to boost your SEO and engagement.

Guest blogging is a powerful strategy for blog growth and SEO. Writing articles for other blogs in your niche can help you reach a wider audience and earn high-quality backlinks. Guest blogging allows you to showcase your expertise and build relationships with other bloggers and influencers. To get started, identify reputable blogs in your niche and pitch them relevant and valuable content ideas. Writing high-quality guest posts can enhance your blog's SEO and attract more readers.

Promoting your blog posts is crucial for increasing their visibility and attracting more traffic. Sharing your content on social media platforms, sending it to your email list, and reaching out to influencers and bloggers can increase its reach. Using paid advertising, such as social media ads and Google Ads, can also boost your content's visibility. Effective content promotion amplifies your reach, attracts more traffic, and improves your SEO. Promoting your blog posts ensures they reach your target audience and drive more traffic to your site.

Content calendars are essential for planning and organizing your blog's content. A content calendar helps you schedule and plan your blog posts in advance, ensuring you consistently publish new and relevant content. It can include details such as content topics, formats, publication dates, and promotional strategies. Using a content calendar helps you stay organized and ensures your blog's content strategy is focused and effective. Regularly reviewing and updating your content calendar ensures your blog's growth and SEO efforts remain aligned with your goals.

Repurposing content involves reusing and repackaging your existing content in different formats. This can help you reach a wider audience and maximize the value of your content. For example, you can turn a blog post into a video, an infographic, or a podcast episode. Repurposing content allows you to present the same information in different ways, catering to different audience preferences. It also helps you save time and resources by making the most of your existing content. Repurposing content enhances your blog's growth and SEO efforts.

Creating evergreen content is important for long-term blog growth and SEO. Evergreen content addresses timeless topics that continue to attract traffic long after it's published. Examples include how-to guides, tutorials, and FAQs. Creating evergreen content provides ongoing value to your readers and continues to drive traffic to your blog. Focusing on evergreen topics ensures your blog remains relevant and valuable over time. Evergreen content is a smart strategy for sustained blog growth and SEO success.

Social media can enhance your blog's growth and SEO by increasing the visibility of your content and attracting more traffic. Sharing your blog posts on social media platforms can attract attention and encourage others to share them. Engaging with your audience through comments, likes, and shares can build your social media presence and drive more traffic to your blog. Using social media effectively can amplify your blog's reach and improve your search visibility.

Email marketing is an effective way to promote your blog and engage with your audience. Sending newsletters, updates, and promotional emails can drive traffic to your blog and improve your SEO. Building a strong email list and regularly sending valuable content to your subscribers can enhance your blog's growth. Email marketing allows you to reach your audience directly and keep them informed about your latest blog posts and offers. Integrating email marketing into your blog's content strategy can amplify your reach and improve your search visibility.

Tracking blog SEO performance helps you understand the effectiveness of your optimization efforts. Using tools like Google Analytics, Google Search Console, and SEO tools, you can monitor your traffic, keyword rankings, and user engagement. This data helps you identify areas for improvement and optimize your blog for better performance. Regularly reviewing your blog SEO performance ensures your efforts are focused and aligned with your goals. Blog SEO performance analysis is essential for staying competitive and improving your search visibility.

Case studies of successful blog growth and SEO strategies provide valuable insights and inspiration. Analyzing how other bloggers have achieved success with their SEO efforts can help you refine your own strategy. Look for case studies that highlight different aspects of blog SEO, such as keyword research, content creation, or social media promotion. Learning from real-world examples helps you understand best practices and avoid common pitfalls. Applying these lessons to your own strategy can improve your blog's growth and overall performance.

Common blog SEO mistakes to avoid include keyword stuffing, duplicate content, and ignoring user engagement. Ensuring your content is optimized for relevant keywords, original, and engaging is crucial for blog SEO. Regularly auditing your blog and fixing any issues can help maintain your rankings. Staying updated with best practices and algorithm changes is also important. By avoiding common mistakes and following best practices, you can enhance your blog's SEO and improve your site's visibility.

The future of blog SEO involves staying updated with industry trends and advancements in technology. As search engines continue to evolve, it's important to adapt your blog's SEO strategy to stay competitive. Focusing on providing value to your readers, using responsive design, and optimizing for mobile users ensures your blog's SEO efforts remain effective. Staying informed about changes in search algorithms and best practices helps you maintain your online presence. The future of blog SEO involves a more user-focused and data-driven approach.

Tools for blog SEO, such as Google Analytics, Google Search Console, and SEO tools, can enhance your efforts. These tools provide valuable insights, track performance, and help you implement effective blog SEO strategies. Using tools effectively can streamline your blog's SEO process and improve your results. Leveraging technology and data can give you a competitive edge in blog SEO. Investing in the right tools helps you measure and analyze your blog's SEO performance more effectively.

Integrating blog SEO into your overall SEO strategy involves aligning your efforts with your broader SEO goals. This includes optimizing your content, site structure, and technical elements for both desktop and mobile searches. Ensuring your SEO strategy is comprehensive and includes blog SEO helps you reach a wider audience and improve your search visibility. Regularly reviewing and adjusting your strategy based on performance data ensures your efforts are effective and aligned with your goals. A holistic approach to SEO that includes blog SEO is essential for long-term success.

To sum up, SEO for blog growth involves optimizing your blog to attract more traffic, engage your audience, and build your brand. By implementing effective strategies and staying updated with best practices, you can improve your search visibility, drive more traffic to your site, and grow your blog. Focusing on keyword research, content creation, promotion, and performance tracking ensures your blog's SEO efforts are effective and aligned with your goals. Regularly measuring and optimizing your blog's SEO performance helps you stay competitive and achieve better results. Blog SEO is crucial for long-term success and online growth.

Chapter 15: Advanced SEO Techniques

Advanced SEO techniques involve implementing more complex and sophisticated strategies to improve your site's search visibility and performance. These techniques go beyond the basics and require a deeper understanding of SEO principles and best practices. By leveraging advanced SEO techniques, you can gain a competitive edge, attract more traffic, and achieve better results. Understanding how to implement advanced SEO techniques can enhance your online presence and provide a better experience for your users.

Technical SEO audits are essential for identifying and fixing issues that may impact your site's performance. A technical SEO audit involves reviewing all aspects of your site's infrastructure, including site speed, mobile-friendliness, site architecture, and crawlability. Using tools like Google Analytics, Google Search Console, and SEO tools can help you identify technical issues and optimize your site. Regularly conducting technical SEO audits ensures your site meets best practices and provides a seamless experience for users.

Site speed optimization is crucial for providing a good user experience and improving your rankings. Faster sites provide a better user experience and are more likely to rank higher. Optimizing site speed involves compressing images, leveraging browser caching, reducing server response times, and minimizing CSS and JavaScript files. Using tools like Google PageSpeed Insights and GTmetrix can help you identify areas for improvement and optimize your site for faster loading times. Ensuring your site loads quickly improves your search visibility and keeps users engaged.

Mobile optimization is essential in today's digital landscape, as more people use smartphones and tablets to browse the web. Ensuring your site is mobile-friendly with a responsive design, fast loading times, and easy navigation is crucial for mobile SEO. Google uses mobile-first indexing, which means it primarily uses the mobile version of your site for ranking and indexing. Regularly reviewing and updating your mobile site ensures it meets Google's standards and provides a seamless experience for users.

Structured data, or schema markup, helps search engines understand the content on your site better. Using structured data, you can provide additional information about your content, such as product details, reviews, and events. This helps search engines display rich snippets in search results, which can improve your click-through rates and visibility. Implementing structured data involves adding specific code to your pages that tells search engines what the content is about. Properly using structured data enhances your search presence and provides more detailed information to users.

Advanced keyword research involves identifying high-value keywords that can drive more traffic and conversions. This includes researching long-tail keywords, question-based keywords, and transactional keywords that indicate purchase intent. Using tools like Ahrefs, SEMrush, and Moz can help you find valuable keywords and analyze their competition and search volume. Regularly updating your keyword research ensures your content remains relevant and competitive.

Content clusters and topic clusters are advanced content strategies that involve organizing your content around central themes or topics. This involves creating pillar content that covers a broad topic and supporting content that dives deeper into specific subtopics. Using internal links to connect related content helps search engines understand the structure and hierarchy of your content. Content clusters improve your site's organization and provide a better user experience. Implementing content clusters enhances your content strategy and improves your search visibility.

Voice search optimization is an essential aspect of modern SEO, as more people use voice assistants like Siri, Alexa, and Google Assistant to search the web. Voice search queries are typically longer and more conversational than text searches, requiring a different approach to optimization. By optimizing your site for voice search, you can improve your visibility and reach a broader audience. Understanding how voice search works and implementing effective strategies can enhance your SEO and provide a better user experience.

International SEO involves optimizing your site for different languages and regions. This is important if you have a global audience or operate in multiple countries. Using hreflang tags, creating localized content, and optimizing for local search engines can enhance your international SEO. Hreflang tags tell search engines which language and region a page is intended for, helping them deliver the right content to users. Properly implementing international SEO can improve your site's visibility and reach a broader audience.

Link reclamation involves identifying and reclaiming lost or broken backlinks. This can happen when a page is deleted or moved, causing the link to return a 404 error. Using tools like Ahrefs and SEMrush, you can identify broken backlinks and reach out to the site owners to request a link update. Reclaiming lost backlinks helps maintain your backlink profile and improve your search visibility. Link reclamation is an effective strategy for preserving the value of your existing backlinks and enhancing your SEO.

Content gap analysis helps you identify content opportunities and gaps in your existing strategy. This involves analyzing your competitors' content to find topics and keywords you may be missing. Using tools like Ahrefs, SEMrush, and Moz, you can identify content gaps and create new content to fill those voids. Content gap analysis ensures your content strategy is comprehensive and aligned with your audience's needs. Addressing content gaps enhances your SEO and provides more value to your users.

Advanced link-building strategies involve earning high-quality backlinks from reputable sources. This includes techniques like broken link building, guest blogging, and influencer outreach. Broken link building involves finding broken links on other websites and offering your content as a replacement. Guest blogging allows you to write articles for other blogs in your niche and include links back to your site. Influencer outreach involves connecting with influencers in your niche and encouraging them to share or link to your content. Implementing advanced link-building strategies enhances your backlink profile and improves your search visibility.

Conversion rate optimization (CRO) involves improving your site's ability to convert visitors into customers or leads. Using tools like Google Analytics, Optimizely, and Unbounce, you can track conversions and identify areas for improvement. CRO involves analyzing user behavior, testing different elements, and optimizing your site for better performance. Regularly reviewing your conversion data ensures your site is effective at achieving your goals. Conversion rate optimization is essential for maximizing the value of your traffic and improving your site's performance.

A/B testing involves comparing two versions of a page or element to see which performs better. Using tools like Optimizely, VWO, and Google Optimize, you can run A/B tests on different elements of your site, such as headlines, images, and calls to action. A/B testing helps you understand which changes improve user engagement and conversions.

Regularly conducting A/B tests ensures your site is optimized for better performance. A/B testing is a valuable tool for improving your SEO and user experience.

SEO automation involves using tools and software to streamline and automate your SEO tasks. This includes tasks like keyword research, rank tracking, and reporting. Using tools like Ahrefs, SEMrush, and Moz, you can automate your SEO processes and save time and resources. SEO automation helps you manage your SEO strategy more efficiently and focus on high-value tasks. Implementing SEO automation enhances your productivity and improves your SEO performance.

Competitor analysis helps you understand how your site compares to others in your niche. Using tools like Ahrefs, SEMrush, and Moz, you can analyze your competitors' backlinks, keyword rankings, and content. This data helps you identify opportunities for improvement and refine your strategy. Regularly reviewing your competitor analysis ensures your site stays competitive and aligned with industry trends. Competitor analysis is essential for understanding your strengths and weaknesses and improving your SEO performance.

Content audits involve reviewing and analyzing your existing content to identify opportunities for improvement. This includes evaluating your content's performance, relevance, and quality. Using tools like Google Analytics, Google Search Console, and SEO tools, you can conduct a comprehensive content audit and optimize your content for better performance. Regularly conducting content audits ensures your content remains relevant, valuable, and aligned with your audience's needs. Content audits are essential for maintaining a high-quality content strategy and improving your SEO.

Link intersect analysis helps you identify sites that link to your competitors but not to you. Using tools like Ahrefs and SEMrush, you can conduct a link intersect analysis and find opportunities to earn backlinks from these sites. This involves reaching out to the site owners and offering valuable content or collaboration opportunities. Link intersect analysis helps you expand your backlink profile and improve your search visibility. Implementing link intersect analysis enhances your link-building strategy and provides more value to your users.

Voice search and e-commerce are closely connected, as more people use voice assistants to search for products and make purchases. Optimizing your e-commerce site for voice search involves using natural language, answering common questions, and providing detailed product information. Ensuring your site is mobile-friendly and optimized for local search can also improve your voice search rankings. Voice search optimization for e-commerce helps you reach more customers and improve your sales.

Tracking advanced SEO metrics helps you understand the effectiveness of your optimization efforts. Important metrics include organic traffic, keyword rankings, bounce rate, time on site, and conversions. Using tools like Google Analytics, Google Search Console, and SEO tools, you can track your advanced SEO metrics and make informed decisions. Regularly reviewing your advanced SEO metrics ensures your strategy is effective and aligned with your goals. Tracking advanced SEO metrics is essential for maintaining and improving your search visibility.

Case studies of advanced SEO techniques provide valuable insights and inspiration. Analyzing how other sites have achieved success with their advanced SEO efforts can help you refine your own strategy. Look for case studies that highlight different aspects of advanced SEO, such as technical audits, content clusters, or international SEO. Learning from real-world examples helps you understand best practices and avoid common pitfalls. Applying these lessons to your own strategy can improve your advanced SEO and overall performance.

Common advanced SEO mistakes to avoid include over-optimization, neglecting user experience, and ignoring technical issues. Ensuring your site is optimized for relevant keywords, user-friendly, and technically sound is crucial for advanced SEO. Regularly auditing your site and fixing any issues can help maintain your rankings. Staying updated with best practices and algorithm changes is also important. By avoiding common mistakes and following best practices, you can enhance your advanced SEO and improve your site's visibility.

The future of advanced SEO involves staying updated with industry trends and advancements in technology. As search engines continue to evolve, it's important to adapt your advanced SEO strategy to stay competitive. Focusing on providing value to your audience, using advanced techniques, and optimizing for user experience ensures your advanced SEO efforts remain effective. Staying informed about changes in search algorithms and best practices helps you maintain your online presence. The future of advanced SEO involves a more sophisticated and user-focused approach.

Tools for advanced SEO, such as Google Analytics, Google Search Console, Ahrefs, SEMrush, and Moz, can enhance your efforts. These tools provide valuable insights, track performance, and help you implement effective advanced SEO strategies. Using tools effectively can streamline your advanced SEO process and improve your results. Leveraging technology and data can give you a competitive edge in advanced SEO. Investing in the right tools helps you measure and analyze your advanced SEO performance more effectively.

Integrating advanced SEO into your overall SEO strategy involves aligning your efforts with your broader SEO goals. This includes optimizing your content, site structure, and technical elements for both desktop and mobile searches. Ensuring your SEO strategy is comprehensive and includes advanced SEO helps you reach a wider audience and improve your search visibility. Regularly reviewing and adjusting your strategy based on performance data ensures your efforts are effective and aligned with your goals. A holistic approach to SEO that includes advanced SEO is essential for long-term success.

To sum up, advanced SEO techniques involve implementing more complex and sophisticated strategies to improve your site's search visibility and performance. By leveraging advanced techniques and staying updated with best practices, you can gain a competitive edge, attract more traffic, and achieve better results. Focusing on technical audits, keyword research, content clusters, and voice search optimization ensures your advanced SEO efforts are effective and aligned with your goals. Regularly measuring and optimizing your advanced SEO performance helps you stay competitive and achieve better results. Advanced SEO is crucial for long-term success and online growth.

www.ingramcontent.com/pod-product-compliance
Lightning Source LLC
Chambersburg PA
CBHW052330220526
45472CB00001B/357